D0930132

On Doing the Right Thing

AND OTHER ESSAYS

ON DOING THE RIGHT THING

AND OTHER ESSAYS

by

Albert Jay Nock

Essay Index Reprint Series

 BOOKS FOR LIBRARIES PRESS
FREEPORT, NEW YORK

INTERNATIONAL STANDARD BOOK NUMBER:
0-8369-2006-6

LIBRARY OF CONGRESS CATALOG CARD NUMBER:
76-128282

PRINTED IN THE UNITED STATES OF AMERICA

To C. R. W.

CONTENTS

▼

Preface

*T*HESE essays, except the first, were published in *Harper's Magazine* and *The American Mercury* within the last three years; the first one was printed as an introduction to a small volume, published in 1924 by A. and C. Boni, of selections from the writings of Artemus Ward. My best thanks are due Messrs. Boni and the editors of *Harper's* and the *Mercury* for permission to reprint them.

They bear on various aspects of the same subject, namely, the quality of civilization in the United States; and hence they have a certain unity, or a certain monotony, according as one is disposed to regard them. They are reprinted as they first appeared, without any changes worth speaking of. The exigencies of magazine publication, chiefly the haunting terror of a space limit, has had its effect upon their continuity and completeness, and to some extent upon their manner, as well. But a little im-

agination and benevolence will, I think, supply
a sense of the integrity of critical purpose behind them.

ALBERT JAY NOCK.

Brussels, 27 March, 1928.

On Doing the Right Thing

Artemus Ward[1]

CHARLES FARRAR BROWNE, known to the world as Artemus Ward, was born ninety years ago in Waterford, Maine. He died at an age when most of us are only beginning to mature—thirty-three. Little more can be told of him by way of formal biography. Mr. Don C. Seitz lately employed himself upon a labour of love by seeking out and publishing all that is known, probably, of the externalities of Ward's life. Mr. Seitz has made the most of what was put before him, and in so doing he has done good service to the history of American letters; yet one closes his fine volume with a keen sense of how little he had to do with, a sense of the slightness and insignificance of his material. All Ward's years were *Wanderjahre*; he had no schooling, he left a poor rural home at sixteen to work in neighbouring printing-offices; he tramped West and South as a compositor and reporter; he wrote a little, lec-

[1] This essay was printed as the introduction to a volume of *Selected Works of Artemus Ward*, published in 1924 by A. and C. Boni.

I

tured a little, gathered up odds and ends of his writings and dumped them in a woeful mess upon the desk of Carleton, the publisher, to be brought out in two or three slender volumes; he went to New York, then to London, saw as much of collective human life in those centres as he had energy to contemplate; he wrote a few pages for the old *Vanity Fair* and for *Punch,* gave a few lectures in Dodworth Hall on Broadway and Egyptian Hall on Piccadilly; and then he died. Little enough of the *pars magna fui* is to be found here for the encouragement of a biographer; Mr. Seitz, I repeat, is to be congratulated on his intrepidity. It is surely a remarkable thing that one whose experience was limited by the span of thirty-three years, whose literary output was correspondingly scanty, and whose predicable hold upon the future was as slight and hazardous as Mr. Seitz shows Ward's to have been, should have managed to live nearly a century; and it is perhaps more remarkable that he should have done it in a civilization like ours, which is not over-careful with literary reputations and indeed does not concern itself deeply with spiritual achievement or spiritual activity of any kind.

Yet that is what Artemus Ward has some-how managed to do, and Mr. Seitz is on hand with a bibliography of eighteen pages, closely printed in small type, to prove it. Some meas-ure of proof, too, is probably to be found in the fact that a new issue of Ward's complete works came out in London two years ago, and that an American firm has taken thought to publish this present volume. How, then, has Ward contrived to live so long? As a mere fun-maker, it is highly improbable that he could have done it. Ward is officially listed as the first of the great American humorists; Mr. Albert Payson Terhune even commemorates him as the man "who taught Americans to laugh." This is great praise; and one gladly acknowledges that the humorists perform an immense public service and deserve the most handsome public recognition of its value. In the case of Ward, it is all to Mr. Terhune's credit that he perceives this. Yet as one reads Ward's own writings, one is reminded that time's processes of sifting and shaking-down are inexorable, and one is led to wonder whether, after all, in the quality of sheer humorist, Artemus Ward can quite account for his own persistent longevity. In point of the power sheerly to provoke laughter, the power sheerly to amuse, distract and entertain, one doubts that Ward can be said so far to transcend his predecessors, Shillaber and Derby. In point of wit and homely wisdom, of the insight and shrewdness which give substance and momentum to fun-making, it would seem that Ward's contemporary, Henry W. Shaw, perfectly stands comparison with him. The disparity, at all events, is by no means so obvious as to enable one to say surely that the law of the survival of the fittest must take its course in Ward's favour. One is therefore led to suspect either that Ward's longevity is due to some quality which he possessed apart from his quality as humorist, some quality which has not yet, perhaps, been singled out and remarked with sufficient definiteness, or else that it is due to the blind play of chance.

Several considerations tell against the hypothesis of accident. It might be enough to say flatly that such accidents do not happen, that the passing stream of printed matter is too full and swift to permit any literary flotsam to escape being caught and swept on to oblivion by

its searching current. Two other considerations, however, may be remarked as significant.
First, that Ward very soon passed over—almost
immediately passed over, the transition beginning even in the last few months of his life—
passed over from being a popular property to
become a special property of the intelligent and
civilized minority; and he has remained their
special property ever since. In his quality of
humorist he could hardly have done this. Even
had he really been the man who taught
Americans to laugh, disinterested gratitude
could hardly be carried so far. Artemus Ward
himself declined to weep over the memory of
Cotton Mather, saying simply that "he's bin
ded too lengthy"; and such, more or less, are
we all, even the intelligent and civilized among
us. Ward was, in his time, a popular property
in virtue of his singularly engaging personality,
his fine and delicate art as a public speaker and
his brilliant dealing with questions and affairs
of current interest. But his presence is no longer
among us, and the affairs of profoundest public interest in his day are hardly as much as
a memory in ours. No power of humour in
dealing with those affairs could serve to con-

5

tinue him as a cherished property of the intelligent, any more than it could serve to restore him as a popular property now that those affairs, and the interest that they evoked, have disappeared. His continuance must be accounted for by another quality than those which he shared with his predecessors and contemporaries who have not taken on a like longevity.

The second consideration is that Ward has always been the object of a different and deeper regard in England, where his humour is alien, than in America where it is native. It has long been difficult to get a copy of his complete works in this country, even at second hand; the last edition was published by Dillingham in 1898. In London one buys them over the counter, and I think one has always been able to do so. Since the Dillingham edition, Ward has been kept alive in America chiefly in edited issues like Mr. Clifton Johnson's, of 1912, and this present volume; and also in anthologies and in essays by many hands. These have, however, I think invariably, presented him as a humorist, and without taking account of the quality which has given his work the vitality that it seems to possess. The English writers

6

have done, on the whole, rather better; but even they did not strike straight through to this quality, disengage it from those that made up his strictly professional character, and hold it out in clear view; though there is evidence that they themselves had glimpses of it. They were for the most part content, like Ward's own countrymen, to accept him as a humorist and to assume that he kept his place in literature on the strength of his humour; and they were not aware, apparently, that this assumption left them with a considerable problem on their hands. Mr. Seitz quotes Ward's own view of the quality that gives power and permanence to his work—I too shall quote it presently, as it is admirably explicit—and oddly enough, without perceiving that it leaves him with a considerable problem on *his* hands; a problem which, if he had attended to it, might have caused him to change the direction of about three-fourths of his book.

No, clearly it is not by the power of his humour that Ward has earned his way in the world of letters, but by the power of his criticism. Ward was a first-class critic of society; and he has lived for a century by precisely the same

7

power that gave a more robust longevity to Cervantes and Rabelais. He is no Rabelais or Cervantes, doubtless; no one would pretend that he is; but he is eminently of their glorious company. Certainly Keats was no Shakespeare, but as Matthew Arnold excellently said of him, he is *with* Shakespeare; to his own degree he lives by grace of a classic quality which he shares with Shakespeare; and so also is Ward with Rabelais and Cervantes by grace of his power of criticism.

Let us look into this a little, for the sake of making clear the purpose for which this book is issued. I have already said that Ward has become a special property, and that he can never again be a popular property, at least until the coming of that millennial time when most of our present dreams of human perfectability are realized. I have no wish to discourage my publishers, but in fairness I have had to remind them that this delectable day seems still, for one reason or another, to be quite a long way off, and that meanwhile they should not put any very extravagant expectations upon the sale of this volume, but content themselves as best they may with the consciousness that they are serving a

8

vital interest, really the ultimate interest, of the saving Remnant. Ward is the property of an order of persons—for order is the proper word, rather than class or group, since they are found quite unassociated in any formal way, living singly or nearly so, and more or less as aliens, in all classes of our society—an order which I have characterized by using the term *intelligence*. If I may substitute the German word *Intelligenz*, it will be seen at once that I have no idea of drawing any supercilious discrimination as between, say, the clever and the stupid, or the educated and the uneducated. *Intelligenz* is the power invariably, in Plato's phrase, to see things as they are, to survey them and one's own relations to them with objective disinterestedness, and to apply one's consciousness to them simply and directly, letting it take its own way over them uncharted by prepossession, unchannelled by prejudice, and above all uncontrolled by routine and formula. Those who have this power are everywhere; everywhere they are not so much resisting as quietly eluding and disregarding all social pressure which tends to mechanize their processes of observation and thought. Rabelais's first words are words of jovial address,

9

under a ribald figure, to just this order of persons to which he knew he would forever belong, an order characterized by *Intelligenz*; and it is to just this order that Ward belongs.

The critical function which spirits like Ward perform upon this unorganized and alien order of humanity is twofold; it is not only clearing and illuminating, but it is also strengthening, reassuring, even healing and consoling. They have not only the ability but the *temper* which marks the true critic of the first order; for, as we all know, the failure which deforms and weakens so much of the able second-rate critic's work is a failure in temper. Take, for example, by way of a comparative study in social criticism, Rabelais's description of the behaviour of Diogenes at the outbreak of the Corinthian War, and put beside it any piece of anti-militarist literature that you may choose; put beside it the very best that M. Rolland or Mr. Norman Angell or even Count Tolstoy himself can do. How different the effect upon the spirit! Or again, consider in the following pages the pictures which Ward draws of the village of Baldwinsville under stress of the Civil War. Not one item is missing of all that afflicted the person of *Intelligenz* in every community at some time in the last ten years. Ward puts his finger as firmly as Mr. Bertrand Russell and Mr. H. L. Mencken have put theirs, upon all the meanness, low-mindedness, greed, viciousness, bloodthirstiness, and homicidal mania that were rife among us—and upon their exciting causes as well—but the person of *Intelligenz* turns to him, and instead of being further depressed, as Mr. Russell and Mr. Mencken depress him, instead of being further overpowered by a sense that the burdens put upon the spirit of man are greater than it can bear, he is lifted out of his temporary despondency and enervation by a sight of the long stretch of victorious humanity that so immeasurably transcends all these matters of the moment. Such is the calming and persuasive influence of the true critical temper, that one immediately perceives Ward to be regarding all the untowardness of Baldwinsville *sub specie æternitatis,* and one gratefully submits to his guidance towards a like view of one's own circumstances.

The essential humanity of Abraham Lincoln, may be largely determined in one's own mind,

I think, by the fact that he made just this use of Artemus Ward. Mr. Seitz tells us how, in the darkest days of the Civil War, Lincoln read the draft of his Emancipation Proclamation at a special meeting of his Cabinet, and, to the immense scandal and disgust of his associates, prefaced it by reading several pages from Ward. The incident is worth attention for the further establishment of the distinction drawn among men by the quality of *Intelligenz*. Seward, Chase, Stanton, Blair, had ability, they had education; but they had not the free, disinterested play of consciousness upon their environment, they did not instinctively tend to see things as they are, they thought largely by routine and formula, they were pedantic, *unintelligent*—that is precisely the word that Goethe, the greatest of critics, would have applied to them at once. Upon them then, naturally, Lincoln's performance made the impression of mere impudent levity; and thus one is directly led to see great force in Ward's sly suggestion that Lincoln should fill up his Cabinet with showmen! Alas! how often the civilized spirit is moved to wish that the direction of public affairs might be taken out of the hands of those

12

who in their modesty are fond of calling themselves "practical" men, and given over to the
artists, to those who at least have some theoretical conception of a satisfying technique of
living, even though actually they may have
gone no great way in the mastery of its practice.

In another place Mr. Seitz tells us how the
great and good John Bright, the Moses of
British political liberalism, attended one of
Ward's lectures in London, sat gravely through
it, and then observed that "its information was
meagre, and presented in a desultory, discon-
nected manner"! The moment I read that, I
laid down the book, saying to myself, *Behold
the reason for liberalism's colossal failure!* The
primary failure of liberalism is just the failure
in *Intelligenz* that we see so amusingly indicated in the case of Mr. Bright; its secondary
failure, as we saw in the case of the late Mr.
Wilson, for example, is a failure in the high and
sound character that depends so largely upon
Intelligenz for its development. Can one
imagine that Ward would be more intelligible
to representative British liberals since Bright's
day, or that he would make a more serious and
salutary impression upon the energumens who

in this country are busily galvanizing some of
Mr. Wilson's political formulas into a ghastly
simulacrum of life, and setting them up as the
soul and essence of liberalism—upon ex-Jus-
tice Clarke, for example, or ex-Secretary Baker
or Mr. George Foster Peabody?   One smiles at
the thought of it.

Ward said of writers like himself that "they
have always done the most toward helping virtue on its pilgrimage, and the truth has found
more aid from them than from all the grave
polemists and solid writers that have ever
spoken or written. . . . They have helped the
truth along *without encumbering it with themselves*."   I venture to italicize these remarkable
words.   How many good causes there are, to
be sure, that seem hopelessly condemned and
nullified by the personality of those who pro-
fess them!   One can think of any number of
reforms, both social and political, that one
might willingly accept if only one need not accept their advocates too.   Bigotry, arrogance,
intolerance, self-assurance, never ran higher
over public affairs than in Ward's day, yet he
succeeded in putting upon all public questions
the precise critical estimate that one puts upon

14

them now in the perspective of fifty years; its
correspondence with the verdict of history is ex-
traordinarily complete. It would be nothing
remarkable if one should arrive now at a correct critical estimate of the Negro question, for
example, or of the policy of abolition, or of the
character and qualities of public men of the
day, or of the stock phrases, the catchwords and
claptrap that happened for the time being to be
the stock-in-trade of demagoguery; but it is
highly remarkable that a contemporary should
have had a correct critical estimate of them,
and that he should have given to it an expression so strong and so consistent, and yet so little
encumbered with himself as to be wholly ac-
ceptable.

Really, there are very few of the characteristic and distinctive qualities of American life
that Ward's critical power left untouched. I
read somewhere lately—I think in one of Professor Stuart P. Sherman's deliverances, though
I am not quite sure—that Americans are just
now very much in the mood of self-examina-
tion, and that their serious reading of novelists
like Mr. Sinclair Lewis or Mr. Sherwood An-
derson, and of essayists like Mr. Ludwig Lew-

isohn or Mr. Mencken, is proof that they are in
that mood. I have great doubts of all this; yet
if it be true, I can but the more strongly urge
them to reëxamine the work of a first-rate critic,
who fifty years ago drew a picture of our
civilization that in all essential aspects is still
accurate. Ward represents the ideal of this
civilization as falling in with one only of the
several instincts that urge men onward in the
quest of perfection, the instinct of expansion.
The claim of expansion is abundantly satisfied
by Ward's America; the civilization about him
is cordial to the instinct of expansion, fosters it,
and makes little of the obligation to scrupulousness or delicacy in its exercise. Ward takes due
pride in relating himself properly to the pre-
dominance of this instinct; he says that by strict
attention to business he has "amarsed a handsum
Pittance," and that when he has enough to permit him to be pious in good style, like his
wealthy neighbours, he intends to join the
Baldwinsville church. There is an ideal of
civilized life for you, a conception of the progressive humanization of man in society! For
the claim of instincts other than the instinct of
expansion, Ward's America does nothing. It

does nothing for the claim of intellect and knowledge (aside from purely instrumental knowledge) nothing for the claim of beauty and poetry, the claim of morals and religion, the claim of social life and manners.

Our modern school of social critics might therefore conceivably get profit out of studying Ward's view of American life, to see how regularly he represents it, as they do, as manifesting an extremely low type of beauty, a factitious type of morals, a grotesque and repulsive type of religion, a profoundly imperfect type of social life and manners. Baldwinsville is overspread with all the hideousness, the appalling tedium and enervation, that afflict the sensitive soul of Mr. Sinclair Lewis. The young showman's courtship of Betsy Jane Peasley exhausts its resources of romance and poetry; its *beau ideal* of domesticity is completely fulfilled in their subsequent life together—a life fruitful indeed in certain wholesome satisfactions, but by no means such as a "well-formed mind would be disposed to relish." On the side of intellect and knowledge, Baldwinsville supports the editor of the *Bugle* as contentedly as New York supports Mr. Ochs and Mr. Munsey, and to

17

quite as good purpose; it listens to the school-
master's views on public questions as uncriti-
cally as New York listens to Mr. Nicholas Mur-
ray Butler's, and to quite as good purpose.
Baldwinsville's dominant type of morals is as
straitly legalistic, formal, and superficial as our
own; its dominant type of religion is easily
recognizable as the hard, dogged, unintelligent
fanaticism with which Zenith confronted Mr.
Sinclair Lewis. We easily recognize the "dissi-
dence of Dissent and the protestantism of the
Protestant religion," which now inspires the
Anti-Saloon League, and which informs and
animates the gentle ministrations of the Ku-
Klux Klan.

Thus Ward, in his own excellent phrase, powerfully helps along the truth about civilization
in the United States; and all the more powerfully in that, unlike Mr. Lewis and Mr.
Mencken, he does not so encumber it with himself, so overload it with the dragging weight of
his own propensities, exasperations, repugnances, that his criticism, however accurate and
interesting, is repellant and in the long run in-
effectual. Often, indeed, his most searching
criticism is made by indirection, by the turn

of some phrase that at first strikes one as quite insignificant, or at least as quite irrelevant to any critical purpose; yet when this phrase once enters the mind it becomes pervasive, and one finds presently that it has coloured all one's cast of thought—and this is an effect which only criticism of the very first order can produce. For instance, consider the first sentence that he writes in a letter to his wife from the Athens of America:

DEAR BETSY: I write you this from Boston, "the Modern Atkins" as it is denomyunated, altho I skurcely know what those air.

Nothing but that.   Yet somehow when that little piece of exquisite raillery sinks in, it at once begins to put one into just the frame of mind and temper to meet properly the gentle, self-contained provincialism at which it was directed.   Let the reader experiment for himself. Let him first recall the fearfully hard sledding he had on his way through, say, Mr. Barrett Wendell's *History of American Literature,* or the recent volume of Mrs. Fields's reminiscences; let him remember the groan of distress

that now and then escaped him while reading
Mr. Howells's really excellent novel, *The Rise
of Silas Lapham.* Then with this sentence in
mind, let him try reading any one of the three
books again, and see how differently it will
impress him.

After the same fashion one may make quite
good headway with Mr. Villard's biography of
John Brown if one's spirit is cleared and steadied
by Ward's inimitable critique of "Ossawatomie
Brown, or, the Hero of Harper's Ferry."
Amidst the squalor of our popular plays and
popular literature, one preserves a decent
equanimity by perusing Ward's reviews of East
Side theatricals and of Forrest's "Othello," and
his parodies of the cheap and lurid romances of
his day. Our popular magazines take on a less
repellant aspect when one remembers how, after
three drinks of New England rum, Ward
"knockt a small boy down, pickt his pocket of a
New York *Ledger,* and wildly commenced
readin' Sylvanus Kobb's last Tail." No better
criticism of our ludicrous and distressing perversion of the religious instinct can be found than
in his account of his visit to the Shakers, the
Free Lovers, and the Spiritualists. Never was

20

the depth and quality of routine patriotism
more accurately measured than by this, from
the account of his visit to Richmond after the
surrender:

I met a man today—I am not at liberty to tell
his name, but he is an old and inflooential citizen of
Richmond, and sez he, "Why! we've bin fightin agin
the Old Flag! Lor bless me, how sing'lar!" He
then borrer'd five dollars of me and bust into a
flood of tears.

Again, how effective is Ward's criticism of
the mischievous and chlorotic sentimentalism
to which Americans seem invariably to give
their first allegiance! During the Civil War
the popular regard for motherhood was exploited as viciously as during the last war, or
probably in all wars, and Ward's occasional reflections upon this peculiarly contemptible rou-
tine-process of militarism are more effective
than any indignant fulminations of outraged
common sense; as when he suggests, for instance, that "the song writers air doin' the
Mother bisness rayther too muchly," or as when
in another place he remarks that it seems about

21

time somebody began to be a little sorry for the old man. He touches another fond topic of sentimentalism in his story, which I must quote, of leaving home as a boy to embark in the show business. Where can better criticism than this be found?

You know, Betsy, that when I first commenced my career as a moral exhibitor with a six-legged cat and a Bass drum, I was only a simple peasant child—skurce 15 summers had flow'd over my yoothful hed. But I had sum mind of my own. My father understood this. "Go," he said, "Go, my son, and hog the public!" (he ment "knock 'em," but the old man was allus a little given to slang). He put his withered han' tremblingly onto my hed, and went sadly into the house. I thought I saw tears tricklin' down his venerable chin, but it might hav' been tobacker jooce. He chaw'd.

But I must end these illustrations, which I have been tempted perhaps unduly to multiply and enlarge upon because their author has never yet, as far as I am aware, been brought to the attention of modern readers in the one capacity wherein he appears to me to maintain an open communication with the future—the capacity

of critic.   In conclusion I cannot forbear remarking the spring, the abounding vitality and
gusto, that pervade Ward's work, and pointing
out that here too he is with Rabelais and Cervantes.   The true critic is aware, with George
Sand, that for life to be fruitful, life must be
felt as a *joy;* that it is by the bond of *joy,* not of
happiness or pleasure, not of duty or responsibility, that the called and chosen spirits are kept
together in this world.   There was little enough
of joy going in the society that surrounded
Ward; the sky over his head was of iron and
brass; and there is even perhaps less joy current
in American society now.   But the true critic
has his resources of joy within himself, and the
motion of his joy is self-sprung.   There may be
ever so little hope of the human race, but that
is the moralist's affair, not the critic's.   The
true critic takes no account of optimism or pes-
simism; they are both quite outside his purview; his affair is one only of joyful appraisal,
assessment, and representation.

Epitaphs are notably exuberant, but the simple line carved upon Ward's tombstone presents
with a most felicitous precision and completeness, I think, the final word upon him.   "His

name will live as a sweet and unfading recollection." Yes, just that is his fate, and there is
none other so desirable. *Mansueti possidebunt
terram*, said the Psalmist, the *amiable* shall possess the earth; and so, in the long run, they do.
Insight and wisdom, shrewdness and penetration—for a critic these are great gifts, indispen-
sable gifts, and the public has regard for their
exercise, it gives gratitude for the benefits that
they confer; but they are not enough of themselves to invest a critic's name with the quality
of a sweet and unfading recollection. To do
this they must communicate themselves through
the medium of a *temper*, a prepossessing and
persuasive amiability. Wordsworth showed
himself a great critic when he said of his own
poems that "they will coöperate with the benign
tendencies in human nature and society, and
will in their degree be efficacious in making
men wiser, better, and happier"; and it is just
because of their unvarying coöperation with the
benign tendencies in human nature and society
that Ward's writings have made him in the
deepest sense a possession, a cherished and ennobling possession, of those who know him.

24

The Decline of Conversation

I

T HE more one thinks of it, the more one finds
in Goethe's remark that the test of civilization
is conversation. The common method of rat-
ing the civilization of peoples by what they
have got and what they have done is really a
poor one; for some peoples who have got much
and done a great deal strike one at once as less
civilized than others who have got little and
done little. Prussia, for example, was relatively
a poor State a century ago, while fifteen years
ago it was rich and active; yet one would hardly
say that the later Prussia was as civilized a
country as the Prussia of Frederick's time.
Somewhat the same might be said of Tudor
England and modern England. The civilization of a country consists in the quality of life
that is lived there, and this quality shows plain-
est in the things that people choose to talk about
when they talk together, and in the way they
choose to talk about them.

It can be taken for granted, I suppose, that

25

man has certain fundamental instincts which must find some kind of collective expression in the society in which he lives. The first and fundamental one is the instinct of expansion, the instinct for continuous improvement in material well-being and economic security. Then there is the instinct of intellect and knowledge, the instinct of religion and morals, of beauty and poetry, of social life and manners. Man has always been more or less consciously working towards a state of society which should give collective expression to these instincts. If society does not give expression to them, he is dissatisfied and finds life irksome, because every unused or unanswered instinct becomes a source of uneasiness and keeps on nagging and festering within him until he does something about it. Moreover, human society, to be permanently satisfactory, must not only express all these instincts, but must express them all in due balance, proportion, and harmony. If too much stress be laid on any one, the harmony is interrupted, uneasiness and dissatisfaction arise, and, if the interruption persists, disintegration sets in. The fall of nations, the decay and disappearance of whole civilizations, can be finally

26

interpreted in terms of the satisfaction of these instincts. Looking at the life of existing nations, one can put one's finger on those instincts which are being collectively overdone at the expense of the others. In one nation the instinct of expansion and the instinct of intellect and knowledge are relatively over-developed; in another, the instinct of beauty; in another, the instinct of manners; and so on. The term *symphonic*, which is so often sentimentally applied to the ideal life of society, is really descriptive; for the tendency of mankind from the beginning has been towards a functional blending and harmony among these instincts, precisely like that among the choirs of an orchestra. It would seem, then, that the quality of life in any society means the degree of development attained by this tendency. The more of these instincts that are satisfied, and the more delicate the harmony of their interplay, the higher and richer is the quality of life in that society; and it is the lower and poorer according as it satisfies fewer of these instincts and permits disharmony in their interplay.

American life has long been fair game for the observer. Journalistic enterprise now beats

up the quarry for the foreigner and brings it
in range for him from the moment the ship
docks, or even before; and of late the native
critic has been lending a brisk hand at the sport.
So much, in fact, has been written about the
way we live, how we occupy ourselves, how we
fill up our leisure, the things we do and leave
undone, the things we are likely to do and likely
to leave undone, that I for one would never
ask for another word on such matters from
anybody. As a good American, I try to keep
up with what is written about us, but it has become rather a dull business and I probably miss
some of it now and then, so I cannot say that
no observer has ever made a serious study of
our conversation. In all I have read, however,
very little has been made of the significance of
the things we choose to talk about and our ways
of talking about them. Yet I am sure that
Goethe's method would give a better measure
of our civilization than any other, and that it
would pay any observer to look into it. For
my own part, ever since I stumbled on Goethe's
observation—now more than twenty years ago
—I have followed that method in many lands.
I have studied conversation more closely than

28

any other social phenomenon, picking up from it all the impressions and inferences I could, and I have always found that I got as good results as did those whose critical apparatus was more elaborate. At least, when I read what these critics say about such people as I know, especially my own, they seem to tell me little with which I was not already acquainted.

II

Speaking as Bishop Pontoppidan did about the owls in Iceland, the most significant thing that I have noticed about conversation in America is that there is so little of it, and as time goes on there seems less and less of it in my hearing. I miss even so much of the free play of ideas as I used to encounter years ago. It would seem that my countrymen no longer have the ideas and imagination they formerly had, or that they care less for them, or that for some reason they are diffident about them and do not like to bring them out. At all events the exercise of ideas and imagination has become unfashionable. When I first remarked this phenomenon I thought it might be an illusion of advancing age, since I have come to

29

years when the past takes on an unnaturally attractive colour. But as time went on the fact became unmistakable and I began to take notice accordingly.

As I did so a long-buried anecdote arose to the top of my mind and has remained there ever since. I am reminded of it daily. Years ago Brand Whitlock told me the story of an acquaintance of his—something in the retail clothing way—junior partner in a firm whose name I no longer remember, so for convenience we will make acknowledgments to Mr. Montague Glass and call it Maisener and Finkman. Mr. Finkman turned up at the store one Monday morning, full of delight at the wonderful time he had had at his partner's house the evening before—excellent company, interesting conversation, a supreme occasion in every respect. After dinner, he said—and such a dinner!—"we go in the parlor and all the evening until midnight we sit and talk it business."

Day after day strengthens the compulsion to accept Mr. Finkman as a type. This might be thought a delicate matter to press, but after all, Mr. Finkman is no creation of one's fancy, but on the contrary he is a solid and respectable

30

reality, a social phenomenon of the first importance, and he accordingly deserves attention
both by the positive side of his preferences and
addictions and by the negative side of his distastes. I am farthest in the world from believing that anything should be "done about" Mr.
Finkman, or that he should be studied with an
ulterior view either to his disparagement or his
uplift.   I am unequivocally for his right to an
unlimited exercise of his likes and dislikes, and
his right to get as many people to share them as
he can. All I suggest is that the influence of
his tastes and distastes upon American civilization should be understood. The moment one
looks at the chart of this civilization one sees
the line set by Mr. Finkman, and this line is
so distinct that one cannot but take it as one's
principal lead. If one wishes to get a measure
of American civilization, one not only must
sooner or later take the measure of Mr. Finkman's predilections, but will save time and trouble by taking it at the outset.

As evidence of the reach of Mr. Finkman's
influence on the positive side, I notice that those
of my American acquaintance whose interests
are not purely commercial show it as much as

others. Musicians, writers, painters, and the like seem to be at their best and to entertain themselves best when they "talk it business." In bringing up the other instincts into balance with the instinct of expansion, such persons as these have an advantage, and one would expect to see that advantage reflected in their conversation much more clearly and steadily than it is. Where two or three of them were gathered together, one would look for a considerable play of ideas and imagination, and one would think that the instinct of expansion—since one perforce must give so much attention to it at other times—might gladly be let off on furlough. But I observe that this is seldom the case. For the most part, like Mr. Finkman, these people begin to be surest of themselves, most at ease and interested, at the moment when the instinct of expansion takes charge of conversation and gives it a directly practical turn.

One wonders why this should be so. Why should Mr. Finkman himself, after six days' steady service of the instinct of expansion, be at his best and happiest when he yet "talks it business" on the seventh? It is because he has managed to drive the whole current of his being through the relatively narrow channel set by the instinct of expansion. When he "talks it business," therefore, he gets the exhilarating sense of drive and speed. A millstream might thus think itself of more consequence than a river; probably the Iser feels more importance and exhilaration in its narrow leaping course than the Mississippi in filling all the streams of its delta. By this excessive simplification of existence Mr. Finkman has established the American formula of success. He makes money, but money is his incidental reward; his real reward is in the continuous exhilaration that he gets out of the processes of making it. My friends whose interests are not exclusively commercial feel the authority of the formula and share in the reward of its obedience. My friend A, for example, writes a good novel. His instincts of intellect, beauty, morals, religion, and manners, let us say, all have a hand in it and are satisfied. He makes enough out of it to pay him for writing it, and so his instinct of expansion is satisfied. But he is satisfied, not exhilarated. When, on the other hand, his publisher sells a hundred thousand copies of another novel, he is at once in the American

33

formula of success. The novel may not have much exercised his sense of intellect, beauty, morals, religion, and manners—it may be, in other words, an indifferent novel—but he is nevertheless quite in Mr. Finkman's formula of success and he is correspondingly exhilarated. He has crowded the whole stream of his being into the channel cut by the instinct of expansion, and his sensations correspond to his achievement.

Thus by his positive action in establishing the American formula of success, Mr. Finkman has cut what the Scots call a "monstrous cantle" out of conversation. Conversation depends upon a copiousness of general ideas and an imagination able to marshal them. When one "talks it business," one's ideas may be powerful, but they are special; one's imagination may be vigorous, but its range is small. Hence proceeds the habit of particularizing—usually, too, by way of finding the main conversational staple in personalities. This habit carries over, naturally, into whatever excursions Mr. Finkman's mind is occasionally led to make outside the domain of the instinct of expansion; for his disuse of imagination and general ideas outside this sphere

34

disinclines him to them and makes him unhandy with them. Thus it is that conversation in America, besides its extreme attenuation, presents another phenomenon. On its more serious side it is made up almost entirely of particularization and, on its higher side, of personalities.

These characteristics mark the conversation of children and, therefore, may be held to indicate an extremely immature civilization. The other day a jovial acquaintance who goes out to dinner a good deal told me a story that brings out this point. It seems he had just been hearing bitter complaints from a seasoned hostess who for years has fed various assorted contingents of New York's society at her board. She said that conversation at her dinner-table had about reached the disappearing-point. She had as much trouble about getting her guests into conversation as one has with youngsters at a children's party, and all the conversation she could prod out of them nowadays, aside from personalities, came out in the monotonous minute-gun style of particular declaration and perfunctory assent.

"She's right about that," my friend went on. "Here's a *précis* of the kind of thing I hear evening after evening. We go in to dinner talking personalities, no matter what subject is up. The theatre—we talk about the leading lady's gowns and mannerisms, and her little ways with her first husband. Books—we hash over all the author's rotten press-agentry, from the make of his pajamas to the way he does his hair. Music—we tell one another what a dear love of a conductor Kaskowhisky is, and how superior in all respects to von Bugghaus, whose back isn't half so limber. Damned quacks actually, you know, both of them! Good Lord! man, can you wonder that this country killed Mahler and put Karl Muck in jail?

"Well, we sit down at the table. Personalities taper off with the end of the soup. Silence. Then some puffy old bullfrog of a banker retrieves his nose out of his soup-cup, stiffens up, coughs behind his napkin, and looks up and down the line. 'Isn't it remarkable how responsibility brings out a man's resources of greatness? Now who would have thought two years ago that Calvin Coolidge would ever develop into a great leader of men?'

"*Guests, in unison, acciaccato*—'Uh-huh.'

"Next course. Personalities pick up a little

and presently taper off again. Somebody else
stiffens up and pulls himself together. 'Isn't
it splendid to see the great example that America is setting in the right use of wealth? Just
think, for instance, of all the good that Mr.
Rockefeller has done with his money.'

"*Guests, fastoso*—'Uh-huh.' "

My lively friend may have exaggerated a
little—I hope so—but his report is worth an
observer's careful notice for purposes of comparison with what one hears oneself. His next
remark is worth attention as bringing out still
another specific characteristic of immaturity.

"But what goes against my grain," he continued, "is that if you pick up some of this infernal guff and try to pull it away from the
particular and personal, and to make real conversation of it, they sit on you as if you were
an enemy of society. Start the banker on a
discussion of the idea of leadership—what it
means, what the qualifications for leadership
are, and how far any President can go to fill
the bill—how far any of them has ever gone to
fill it—and all he'll do is to grunt, and say, 'I
guess you must be some sort of a Red, ain't
you?' A bit of repartee like that gets him a

37

curtain call from the rest every time. It's a
fine imaginative lot that I train with, believe
me! I have sat at dinner-tables in Europe with
every shade of opinion, I should say, and in
one way or another they all came out. That's
what the dinner was got up for. How can you
have any conversation if all you are expected to
do is to agree?"

III

It is a mark of maturity to differentiate easily
and naturally between personal or social opposition and intellectual opposition. Everyone
has noticed how readily children transfer their
dislike of an opinion to the person who holds
it, and how quick they are to take umbrage at
a perscn who speaks in an unfamiliar mode or
even with an unfamiliar accent. When the in-
fant-minded Pantagruel met with the Limosin
who spoke to him in a Latinized macaronic
jargon, he listened awhile and then said, "What
devilish language is this?—by the Lord, I think
thou art some kind of heretic." Mr. Finkman's
excessive simplification of life has made anything like the free play of ideas utterly incom-
prehensible to him. He never deals with ideas,

except such limited and practical ones as may help get him something, and he cannot imagine anyone ever choosing, even on occasion, to do differently. When he "talks it business," the value of ideas, ideals, opinions, sentiments, is purely quantitative; putting any other value on them is a waste of time. Under all circumstances, then, he tends to assume that other people measure the value of their ideas and opinions as he does his, and that they employ them accordingly; and hence, like my friend's banker, when some one tries to lead up into a general intellectual sparring for mere points, he thinks he is a dangerous fellow with an ax to grind.

This puts the greatest imaginable restraint upon conversation, a restraint which betrays itself to the eye of the observer in some rather odd and remarkable ways. I have been much interested, for example, to see that the conversion of conversation into mere declaratory particularization has lately been taken up in a commercial way. One reads advertisements of enterprising people who engage to make you shine in conversation. They propose to do this by loading you up with a prodigious number of facts of all kinds, which you can fire off at will from the machine-gun of your memory. On this theory of conversation, a statistician with Macaulay's memory is the ideal practitioner of social amenities; and so indeed, with Mr. Finkman's sensibilities in view, he would be.

Another odd manifestation of this restraint is the almost violent eagerness with which we turn to substitutes for conversation in our social activities. Mr. Finkman must not be left alone in the dark with his apprehensions a moment longer than necessary. After such a dinner as my debonair friend described, it is at once necessary to "do something"—the theatre, opera, cabaret, dancing, motoring, or what not—and to keep on doing something as long as the evening lasts. It is astonishing to see the amount of energy devoted to keeping out of conversation; "doing something" has come to be a term of special application. Almost every informal invitation reads, "to dinner, and then we'll do something." It is even more astonishing to see that this fashion is followed by persons whose intelligence and taste are sufficient, one would think, to put them above it. Quite often

40

one finds oneself going through this routine
with persons quite capable of conversation, who
would really rather converse, but who go
through it apparently because it is the thing to
go through. When this happens, one marvels
at the reach and the authority of Mr. Finkman's
predilections—yet there they are.

My friend was right in saying that conversation is managed differently in Europe. I was
reminded of this not long ago, when the German airship made its great flight to this country.
Everyone remembers the vast amount of public
interest in this event, and how the pilot of the
airship, Doctor Eckener, was fêted and fussed
over from one end of the country to the other.
Three or four days after the landing, a friend
of mine, a German banker, asked me to lunch-
eon at his house. There were four of us—
Doctor Eckener, his assistant, our host, and myself. We talked for something over two hours,
largely about music, a good deal about the
geography and history of the region around
Friedrichshafen, and for half an hour, perhaps,
about European public affairs. From first to
last, not one word was said about the flight of
the airship or about the business of aviation or

41

the banking business. The conversation was wholly objective and impersonal; each one spoke his mind, and none of us felt any pressure towards agreement. I remember that I myself put out some pretty heretical opinions about the structure of music-drama. No one agreed with me, but no one dreamed of transferring to myself the brunt of his objections to my opinion.

This kind of thing gives the impression of maturity, and, as far as my experience goes, it is as common in Europe as it is uncommon here. There has been much comment lately upon the attraction that Europe exerts upon certain American types. I am led to wonder if it be not perchance the attraction of maturity. Children may be delightful, may be interesting, may be ever so full of promise, and one may be as fond of them as possible—and yet when one has them for warp and filling, one must get a bit bored with them now and then, in spite of oneself. I have had little to do with children, so I speak under correction; but I should imagine that one would become bored with their intense simplification of life, their tendency to drive the whole current of life noisily through one channel, their vehement reduction of all

42

values to that of quantity, their inability to take any but a personal view of anything. But just these are the qualities of American civilization as indicated by the test of conversation. They inhere in Mr. Finkman and are disseminated by his influence to the practical exclusion of any other. I can imagine, then, that one might in time come to be tired of them and to wish oneself in surroundings where man is accepted as a creature of "a large discourse, looking before and after," where life is admittedly more complex and its current distributed in more channels—in other words, where maturity prevails.

One is impressed, I think, by the way this difference is repeatedly brought out in ordinary conversation in Europe and America—in the choice of things to talk about and in the way people talk about them. I am impressed by it even in conversation with children, though as I said, due allowance ought to be made for the fact that my experience with children is not large. Yet even so, I do not think it is special or exceptional. I have a friend, for instance, whom I go to see whenever I am in Brussels, and it is the joy of my life to play at sweethearts with his three daughters who range from

seven to sixteen.   My favourite is the middle
one, a weedy and nonchalant charmer of twelve.
She does not impress me as greatly gifted; I
know several American girls who seem naturally
abler.   But in conversation with her I detect a
power of disinterested reflection, an active sense
of beauty, and an active sense of manners, beyond any that I ever detected in American
children; and these contribute to a total effect
of maturity that is agreeable and striking.

IV

An observer passing through America with
his mind deliberately closed to any impressions
except those he received from conversation
could make as interesting a conjectural recon-
struction of our civilization as the palæontolo-
gists with an armful of bones make of a
dinosaur.   He would postulate a civilization
which expresses the instinct of expansion to a
degree far beyond anything ever seen in the
world, but which does not express the instinct of
intellect and knowledge, except as regards instrumental knowledge, and is characterized by
an extremely defective sense of beauty, a defective sense of religion and morals, a defective

sense of social life and manners. Its institutions reflect faithfully this condition of excess and defect. A very brief conversation with Mr. Finkman would enable one to predicate almost precisely what kind of schooling he considered an adequate preparation for life, what kind of literature he thought good enough for one to read, plays for one to see, architecture to surround oneself with, music to listen to, painting and sculpture to contemplate. It would be plain that Mr. Finkman had succeeded in living an exhilarating life from day to day without the aid of any power but concentration—without reflection, without ideas, without ideals, and without any but the most special emotions—that he thought extremely well of himself for his success, and was disposed to be jealous of the peculiar type of institutional life which had enabled it or conduced to it. The observer, therefore, would postulate a civilization marked by an extraordinary and inquisitional intolerance of the individual and a corresponding insistence upon conformity to pattern. For in general, it is reflection, ideas, ideals, and emotions that set off the individual, and with these Mr. Finkman has had nothing to do; he has got on without them to what he considers success, and hence he sees no need of them, distrusts them, and thinks there must be a screw loose with the individual who shows signs of them.

There is a pretty general consensus among observers that this picture corresponds in most respects with the actual civilization of the United States, and many of them deplore the correspondence. I do not deplore it. It seems to me important that Mr. Finkman should have room according to his strength, that he should be unchecked and unhampered in directing the development of American civilization to suit himself. I believe it will be a most salutary experiment for the richest and most powerful nation in the world to give a long, fair, resolute try-out to the policy of living by the instinct of expansion alone. If the United States cannot make a success of it, no nation ever can, and none, probably, will ever attempt it again. So when critics denounce our civilization as barbarous, I reply that, if so, a few generations of barbarism are a cheap price for the result. Besides, Mr. Finkman may prove himself right; he may prove that man can live a full and satisfying inner life without intellect, with-

46

out beauty, without religion and morals, and with but the most rudimentary social life and manners, provided only he has unlimited exercise of the instinct of expansion, and can drive ahead in the expression of it with the whole force of his being.   If Mr. Finkman proves this, he will have the laugh on many like myself who at present have the whole course of human history behind our belief that no such thing can be done.   But this is a small matter.   The important thing is that we should then have a new world peopled by a new order of beings not at all like ourselves, but by no means devoid of interest on that account.   So, whether the result be in success or in failure, the great American experiment—for just this is the great American experiment—seems to me wholly worth while.

On Making Low People Interesting

*H*AVING lived of late in a part of Europe where there is very little doing in the way of English, I went for many months without reading a word in my own tongue. By working in a different set of sequences so long, my mind got a bit away from the familiar ones; it rather slacked off on the English-reading habit, as I suppose any mind that has any flexibility is bound to do. But not thinking about this, I was not conscious of the change while it was going on, and when at the end of a long period I fell heir to a dozen cast-off English novels, I was surprised to find that I approached them a good deal like a stranger. On this account, I suppose, certain features of them seemed more odd and unusual than they would have seemed if I had not so completely broken with the English-reading habit, and broken also so largely with the life which they represented.

Some of these novels were British, some American, and all were recent, several being of the current crop, and none more than a couple of years old, I think. They were all good sellers, and had been much talked about. One feature common to them all was that they dealt with low people. I cannot recall a single character out of the whole lot whom one would not rate as pretty distinctly low. This was all to the good, for low people are a great asset to an artist. He can do more with them than with any other kind, because their lives give him a larger range, being lived in a freer fashion, less subject to external directions and restraints. But what impressed me most was that not one of these low people was interesting. Not one of them had anything which touched off the waiting fancy and imagination of the reader. I take it that an interesting person in literature is just what he is in life. He is the kind of person who powerfully stirs your fancy and imagination, so that you want to go back to him and see him again and again, and keep on seeing him as much as you can. None of these people was like that. Bring one of them to life, and you would not cross the street to meet him or give a button to get acquainted with him. They were all so colourless, in fact, so unsubstantial

49

for literary purposes, that the authors had to be continually helping them out, finding something lively for them to do, creating one striking situation after another, to keep them going. This threw over the story a general air of fictitiousness and unreality which was dissatisfying. One novel, for instance, which dealt with the progress of a hard-fisted, bull-headed English farmer-girl on her way to prosperity, culminated in her acquisition of an illegitimate child. This episode had a touch of embarrassment about it, as of something which did not belong there but had been lugged in by the ears. One might say at first sight that it was put in at a publisher's suggestion, as a gratuitous handful of incense to what Matthew Arnold called "the great goddess Aselgeia." Still, as one thought it over, there was little else for the poor girl to do, little else that was within her competence. If she had been an interesting character she need not have done it. Some one once asked Thackeray whether Becky Sharp actually did or did not "go wrong," and Thackeray replied that, for the life of him, he didn't know.

The only interest that I could discover in

these stories, therefore, was in virtue of various literary devices, some legitimate, ingenious, and workman-like, and others rather ramshackle. There was not a vestige of character-portrayal that was anywhere near above par; no vestige of the art that creates a character interesting in itself, irrespective of plot and dramatic action, powerfully stimulating the reader's fancy and imagination, like the forty Flemish types in Old Breughel's sketch-book—just faces, studies in feature and expression, nothing more—but what faces! Still, as I said, I had been long away from my native life and letters, and did not feel sure of my judgment; so I rummaged around for something to true up by, and finally emerged with a copy of the *Pickwick Papers*.

There are eighty-two characters in that book, not counting those in the inserted stories, which come to sixteen more, I think; say about a hundred, all told. Regarded as folks, nearly all of them are low; and those whom one might not class precisely as low are middling ordinary. Even the virtues of Pickwick himself are prosaic. None of these people would ever set the river afire with his genius or make one's head swim with the elevation of his spirit. The great

51

majority, I think, would be put down at once
as the very riddlings of creation. But how *interesting!*—why, one would walk miles unend-
ing to meet one of them and, having met him,
would haunt him, and delightedly follow him
up and down the earth. Not especially the major characters, either, but those who appear and
disappear in the course of half a page, whose
personalities are so clearly and vividly struck
out in a single paragraph that the reader's fancy
and imagination instantly get their whole measure for life by a kind of flashlight photography.
Think of Mr. Smangle, Pott, Mr. Peter
Magnus, Grummer, Pell, Dowler, Mr. Leo
Hunter, Bantam; think of Bob Sawyer, and of
his landlady, Mrs. Raddle! It is conceded that
Dickens did little with female character and
did not seem interested in it, and this has led
some critics to say that he was not able to do
much with it. I suggest that this assumption
runs hard aground on Mrs. Raddle. But there
those people are, low as they can be, mostly the
sheer scum of the earth, none of them really
doing anything in particular—the book has
hardly any literary machinery even at the outset, and promptly drops what little it starts

52

with. There they are—that is practically all one can say about them, and since they are what they are, it is all one need say.

The *Pickwick Papers*, however, are rather a special kind of literary product. The preface tells us that they are not meant to be the conventional type of novel, but a loosely organized aggregation of individual characters run together on a weak thread of commonplace adventure. So, as well as I could without having the book at hand, I revived my recollections of Dickens's next story, which is in all respects quite the regular thing. *Nicholas Nickleby* has a formal plot, well worked out in plenty of dramatic action, for whatever these devices amount to; other authors have done as well with both, and some better. There, again, it is character, mostly of the very lowest, that gives this book its hold upon the reader's fancy and imagination. Mantalini, Gride, Crummles and his barnstormers, the Kenwigses, Squeers, Noggs, Lillyvick—surely the rarest assortment of utter riff-raff, of sheer human sculch, that was ever raked together between two covers, but *interesting* beyond expression. The plot of *Nicholas Nickleby* might be what it liked, the

53

dramatic action might go this way or that way, and no one would give a penny for the difference. So long as these people are what they are, who cares what they do? Let them stand out and mark time, if they choose, like the characters in *Pickwick*, for all the odds it would make. Imagine some go-getting publisher telling Charles Dickens that to "sustain the human interest," and really to "put the book over with a bang," he ought to get Kate Nickleby in the family way by Sir Mulberry Hawk, and fork in all the biological details of the episode that the law allows!

II

But Dickens is Dickens, and one may not expect the average run of authorship to match him, and certainly one would not wish it to imitate him. One might reasonably expect it to emulate him, however, if indeed character-portrayal be any longer regarded as part of authorship's job. The samples I had been assaying did not show traces of any such effort, so I resolved to look farther into the matter. When I came back into the English-speaking world, therefore, I began to persecute my whole literary acquaintance for points on the status of character-portrayal. Was it by way of becoming a lost art, and if so, why? There seemed to be a complete consensus of opinion that it was. Cultivated amateurs and those whose connection with literature is professional told me that character in current English fiction was becoming standardized into a very few types, and that even those few were vague and vapid. As for my second question, I got various answers which I think may be susceptible of synthesis.

To begin with a rather extreme view, a brisk young acquaintance of mine, who is fond of drawing distinctions in favour of "this generation" and "the modern spirit in art" (probably noticing that I am getting on in years and my critical guns a little honeycombed) tells me that no one cares any more for character-portrayal. This shift in taste is due to "the new psychology"—whatever that is—and the thing nowadays is to produce a kind of literary chart or graph of "what goes on in a person's mind." The acme of achievement in the new art is reached, I believe, when one succeeds in showing by what seems a pretty strictly journalistic method "how he got that way." I speak cautiously about these matters, for I feel uncertain about them, not sure that I understand them very well. Like Artemus Ward, I skurcely kno what those air. As well as I can judge, however, one of the novels in my original exhibit would seem to come somewhere near filling my young friend's bill.

It was rather literally the inside story of the development, if one may call it that, of a young girl of the period, a flapper. This flapper was a filthy little trollop—which I hasten to say is no objection to her, for many great characters in fiction are shocking trollops. A trollop is a first-rate literary property, plenty good enough for anybody as far as she goes; but *qua* trollop, she does not go very far, and a good artist knows it. His literary instinct warns him that in this capacity alone she is worth only about a stickful, nonpareil, on the eighth page, last column. If he wants her to be a real headliner, he must freight her up with something more substantial for literary purposes.

But this young woman was a trollop all the time, twenty-four hours a day, being apparently devoid of any other faculty. She was good

for nothing else. This gave the story a patho-
logical turn—a turn of very special and extremely limited interest, quite ludicrously in-
adequate to the amount of space employed to
tell it. I was reminded by contrast, though the
stories have essentially something in common,
of Bill Nye's story of an omnivorous dog that
he once had, named Entomologist, who ate
some liquid plaster-of-Paris one day, and did
not survive the experiment. Bill held an au-
topsy and salvaged the plaster for a memento,
using it as a paper-weight, with the inscription,
"Plaster cast of Entomologist, taken by himself—interior view." This was as much of a
story as these humble literary properties were
worth, and Bill was enough of a literary artist to
refrain from trying to stretch it. Consequently,
as far as he goes, Entomologist is an interesting
figure; he stirs one's fancy and imagination in
a small way, but an agreeable way, and sets
them at work reconstructing the circumstances
and filling in the details for oneself. A good
artist is one who prods up one's fancy and imagination to do all this sort of work. If the
creator of this flapper had been anything of an
artist, her annals would have amounted to a

paragraph. I think I know what went on in
Mr. Jingle's mind most of the time, quite as
well as if Dickens had psychologized and
analyzed him and delivered long-winded dis-
quisitions on how he got that way.

This may be the logical place to comment on
one general tendency common to the dozen
novels that formed my *corpus vile* for dissec-
tion. They all dealt largely with sex-relations,
usually irregular. Complaint of this tendency
is common enough, but the ground of complaint
never seemed to me well taken, and I always
wondered why so much should be made of bad
reasons for complaining of it when it is just as
easy to propose a good one. Sexual irregulari-
ties are in themselves unobjectionable for literary purposes, as far as I can see, and I think it
is simply silly to pretend a "moral issue" in
their treatment. The real trouble is with the
author's own relation to his subject. An author's own obvious preoccupation with sexual
affairs, regular or irregular—I say obvious, because one can discern it instantly—is objection-
able, for the reason that the amount of actual
literary material which these affairs provide is
never enough to satisfy this preoccupation. It

will not go far in the construction of a novel; and his preoccupation keeps him trying to make it go farther than it will go.

For instance, one of the novels in my exhibit propounded a curious prairie-dog's nest of unwholesome mortals, whose whole existence seemed to be made up of pigging together in joyous squalor through three hundred solid pages. This was the total impression conveyed by the story, and it was most unpleasantly dull. Not a character in the book had the slightest pretension to interest—one listlessly wished they would all go off together down a steep place into the sea and get drowned, like their lineal forefathers of Gadara. A very good story can be made of the antecedents and consequences of any mode or form of concubinage, from marriage up and down, but the actual technique of concubinage itself is not diversified enough to permit a writer to do anything with it worth speaking of. It is too undifferentiated, except for subjective conditions which are not reproducible upon a reader. Except for these conditions, which are potent enough but quite unreproducible upon a third person, living with one woman is almost precisely like living with

59

another—even the standard jokes and cartoons on the subject show that; and if it be so in life, which brings into play all the small interest-provoking accidents of social contact and entourage, the general effect of which also is quite unreproducible, how much more so in literature!

To make the case clearer, let us introduce a couple of parallels from one, by the way, who is the unquestioned master in the art of showing "what goes on in a person's mind"—from Tourgueniev. *First Love*, to begin with, is a story of low people; only one person in it, the narrator, is anything but a very poor affair. The heroine, Zinaïda, is a flapper of seventeen or so. Here you have the real thing in flappers and the real thing in trollops. *Qua* flapper and *qua* trollop, Zinaïda makes the candidates put forward by our contemporary literature look like Confederate money. The bare story is squalid and repulsive; a journalistic report of it would be unreadable. But as Tourgueniev unfolds it, the great goddess Lubricity gets not a single grain of incense. Not one detail is propounded for the satisfaction of prurience.

60

The people, dreadful as they are, and the drama, weighted as it is with all that is unnatural and shocking in Zinaïda and her paramour, are more than interesting; they are profoundly moving, they release a flow of sympathy that effaces all other emotions, and one lays down the book with a sense of being really humanized and bettered by having read it. Let the reader get it in Mrs. Garnett's excellent translation, and experiment for himself. Then let him go even farther, and try *Torrents of Spring*. This is a story of the antecedents and consequences of adultery plus seduction, brought about under inconceivably loathsome circumstances. The three principal characters are detestably low. The foremost among them, Maria Nikolaevna, in my judgment the most interesting woman in the whole range of fiction —what would one not give to see her and talk with her for an hour?—is the world's prize slut, if ever there were one. But the author has not the slightest preoccupation with her sluttishness, and hence he communicates none to the reader, and the great goddess Aselgeia goes begging again.

III

Some of my literary acquaintances whom I have questioned tell me that authors write too fast. Eager to satisfy the market, they do not take time to portray character. I doubt the force of this. Dickens wrote furiously against time all his life. Haste drove him into some pretty indifferent grammar sometimes, and often loosened his constructions. But it never switched him off from a straight drive at the essential features of character. If he sketched an individual in seven strokes, you "get" that individual—you get him all. Those seven are the essential strokes, and you can fill in the rest for yourself without any trouble. In this power of instant penetration to the essential he is like Old Breughel. Haste should not interfere with this power in the modern artist, if he has it. It might make him a little slovenly in his technical expression of the essentials after he has caught them, but it should not impair his ability to catch them. It seems to me, therefore, that this explanation will not wash.

Another said that authorship nowadays did not compose with its eye on the object. Its

62

vision wavered about, sometimes on the object, sometimes on arbitrary formulas of interpretation set by publishing-policy, sometimes on possible liberties to be taken with the reader's mind, and so on. But if an artist's eye wanders, he is aware of it; he tears up his sketch, curses himself once or twice, and starts all over again. He knows at once where the trouble is. If he did not he would be no artist, and should be advised to give up literature and take to something else. This criticism, therefore, amounts to saying that we have no artists, or the chance of any, which I doubt. I doubt it on the strength of collateral evidence presented by some of the novels that I am discussing. Another said that current authorship did not know enough about human beings; its experience was superficial and journalistic, not going deep enough to provide a mature, objective, but kindly insight. There is no doubt something in this, but if so, I suggest that it only moves the problem one step backward. Granted that the author has not enough depth of experience, why does not the instinct of an artist make him bestir himself and get it?

My notion is that the author is not altogether

at fault. It takes more than the man to make an artist; it takes the combination of the man and the moment, the man and the *milieu*. An artist must have models, and for him to have them, the civilization around him must produce them. Old Breughel sketched marvellously interesting faces, but the faces were there for him to sketch; the civilization of Brussels produced them, as it still does—you can see a hundred an hour there, any day. British literature, up to a half-century ago, has been peculiarly rich in interesting character—well, British life was peculiarly rich in it. By all accounts, the London of 1827 was swarming with models for Dickens.

No doubt the modern author might do better than he does, since we all might well do that, but I suggest that he cannot be expected to do inordinately better than the civilization around him provides him the technical means of doing. A physician once told me that smallpox had been so far subdued that a whole generation of physicians had come on who had never seen a case; and if one of them by chance did encounter a stray case, he had nothing but book-learning to meet it with. If an author does

64

not reproduce a character of interesting distinction, it is fair to ask how many such characters he ever saw. If his insight into character is superficial, it is fair to ask how much opportunity his civilization ever gave him for deepening it. If his people—especially his low people, his flappers and trollops, his ragamuffins and adventurers—lack savour and individuality, how many such people has he ever known who actually had more? If his types are few and standardized, how about his practicable models? It is rather significant, I think, that the best work, the most artistic work, in character-portrayal done in America is done upon models furnished by encysted cultures, by people who cleave with obstinate tenacity to their traditional bent, and maintain it against the levelling force of the civilization around them—the Irish, for example, and the Jews. Even so capable and experienced a writer as Willa Cather never succeeded in depicting character as she has done in her last book by going back to a transplanted civilization for available models. Potash and Perlmutter, their bloodthirsty competitors, their operators and finishers, their wives' relations, are all really

65

pretty dreadful people, but what profoundly interesting characters they are, how vivid, brilliant, and individual are their qualities! In actual life, too, they are pretty dreadful people. I sometimes think there will be a record-breaking pogrom in New York some day, and there are occasions even now when the most peace-loving person among us wishes he could send over for a couple of *sotnias* of Cossacks to floor-manage the subway rush. But if one can get on an isle of safety somewhere and survey them, how absorbingly *interesting* they are. Think of Mr. Goldblatt and his son-in-law, of Henry Feigenbaum and, above all, of Uncle Mosha Kronberg!—there is an interesting individual for you, as full of fascinations as a cucumber is of seeds.

I once asked an American portrait-painter, a very good one, how many faces had ever turned up in the day's work that really challenged his artistic insight and penetration, like the innumerable great faces put on the canvas by Maes, Hals, Steen, Rembrandt, Fabritius, Koninck, de Backer, and a host of others. He said perhaps two or three. I know that on my

66

return to America after a long sojourn among Belgian types, the most striking impression made upon me was of the curiously uniform, undistinguished, characterless quality of the faces about me. There were perhaps half a hundred Americans on the ship with me, and for two days after we landed, while I was getting my sea-legs off and becoming used to my surroundings, I kept seeing those people all over New York. It was an extremely odd experience. Of course it was not the same person in any case, but each one of the whole series of resemblances was strong enough to take me in for several minutes. What can a portrait painter do? Similarly, what can a literary artist do?

Moreover, the freemasonry of *was uns alle bändigt, das Gemeine* affects the reading public, as well as the artist, in an unfavorable way. No one can make much out of Dickens without some knowledge of the economic and social life of his day. The appreciation of his power of character-portrayal is largely a matter of the interest bred by general information and general culture. When I saw the play "Potash and Perlmutter" some years ago, I seemed to be the

67

only person in the house who was not a Jew.
I saw it twice more, and remarked the same
phenomenon. I wondered how its power of
character-portrayal, much better felt in the
stories than in the play, of course, affected the
average of the *Goyim;* whether their general
level of culture was high enough to enable them
disinterestedly to appraise it for what it was
worth. Several times, at a period when I was
in a position to do so, I have experimented with
promising young sprigs of the hire learning
who had "specialized in English literature,"
Gott soll hüten, by noting what signs they
showed of sparking up over great examples of
character-portrayal. I never got my investment back. If I got a net of three cents on the
dollar I was as elated as if I had found it in
the street. Since those days, when I have seen
my countrymen pausing before portraits done
by the old Flemish masters, I have wondered
what impression was made upon them by the
faces themselves, as indices of character.

IV

I, therefore, suggest, with all possible delicacy, that hopes of "the great American novel"

68

are extravagant. This art requires great subjects; and the life about us does not provide them. It requires a very special order of correspondence between the artist and his environment; and the life about us does not promote this or even permit it. Our civilization, rich and varied as it may be, is not *interesting;* its general level falls too far below the standard set by the collective experience of mankind. If one points with pride to our endless multiplication of the mechanics of existence, and our incessant unintelligent preoccupation with them, the artist replies that with all this he can do nothing. What he demands is great and interesting character, character that powerfully stirs the fancy and imagination, and a civilization in which such interests are dominant cannot supply it.

Today's newspapers carry an item from one of our mid-Western towns, saying that in a raid on some swindling charlatan the police discovered hundreds of letters from people who were burdened with intolerable tedium, which they declared they would do anything in the world to escape "if only he would advise them

69

how." Yet these people had an available apparatus of comfort and of enjoyment surpassing anything ever seen in the world. No doubt they had movies handy, and money enough to patronize them, since the submerged tenth does not write to frauds. Probably many of them had Ford cars, and radio sets yielding jazz to dance by; probably they were better dressed and fed, and more comfortably housed, than people of a station corresponding to theirs have ever been! But all this did not make for an interesting life; and they knew so little what such a life consisted in, and the terms on which it was to be had, that they turned to this wretched fellow's nostrum, whatever it was, in pathetic and ignorant hope. Their case is common; everyone knows that it is, let him pretend as he chooses. Everyone is aware that the failure of our civilization is precisely this failure in *interest*, for which nothing can make up. Our collective life is not "lived from a great depth of being," but from the surface; and the mark of the collective life is on the individual.

Perhaps our civilization knows how to transform itself; if so, the artist may ultimately have

his chance. Perhaps, again, it is permissible to
see a kind of allegory in the story of the man
who fed his horse on shavings. For some reason, he said, just about as the horse began really
to like them, "it up and died on him."

A Cultural Forecast

WE ARE becoming more or less familiar with the assumption that our immediate cultural prospects are not good. It is the motive of most of the "literature of revaluation," or, as Mr. H. L. Mencken prefers to call it, the *Katzenjammer* literature of the period. As far as the fact is concerned, we may face it frankly. There seems no doubt that it will be a long time before the humane life, as the ages have understood the term, will prevail among us—before our collective life and its institutions will reflect any considerable spiritual activity. Our present collective life, in its ideals and aspirations as well as in its actual practice, is admittedly conducted upon a very low spiritual level. One has only to imagine Plato or Virgil, Dante or Rabelais, contemplating it—souls preeminent in the knowledge and practice of the humane life—and one has no trouble in arriving at the verdict that would be passed upon it by the best reason and spirit of mankind.

Moreover, there are no discernible tendencies
showing promise of a better state of things, at
least within a period short enough to give the
question more than an academic interest for our
day. Those of our grandchildren, if any, who
shall feel within them any vague promptings
towards the humane life will be unlikely to find
the general current setting that way much more
strongly than it does at present.

On the score of fact and truth, therefore, one
has nothing against the prophets who keep as-
siduously telling us all this. Their attitude towards the truth, however, and, by consequence,
their attitude towards our present representative
society, seem a little uncritical. Most of them
appear to expect more of our civilization than
it can possibly give them; and their disappoint-
ment takes shape in irritation and complaint.
This seems historically to have been the chief
trouble with the evangelizing spirit, and the
chief reason why evangelists themselves usually got no great way in the practice of the
humane life, and were, on the whole, rather
unpleasant persons to have around. Criticism
reckons with the causes of things, and it duly
apprehends the length of the course which mat-

ters must run under their propulsion, or even under the force of inertia after those causes are no longer operative. Hence, criticism invariably judges social phenomena according to the strength and inveteracy of the causes that give rise to them. In our early days, for example, about a century ago, a representative of Cincinnati's light and learning said to Mrs. Trollope, "Shakespeare, madame, is obscene; and, thank God, *we* are sufficiently advanced to have found it out." Criticism does not stop with remarking that this man's view of both Cincinnati and Shakespeare was very inept, and that he should have done better. Criticism, properly employing the scientific imagination, examines the beginnings and development of Cincinnati's social life, considers its general character and quality, and its only marvel is that any person bred there should have even heard of Shakespeare, or felt it appropriate to have any opinion at all about him, even a silly one. Again, everyone remembers the great fuss that was made last year over the Treasury Department's confiscation of some imported classic, I have forgotten which one; or only the other day, over Mayor Thompson's *opera-buffa* performances in the Chicago libraries. But con-

74

sidering the progress of our cultural life as exhibited consecutively in the great work of Mr. Beard, or as shown by Mr. Bowers, Mr. Sandburg, Mr. Allan Nevins and Mr. Paxton Hibben, in their study of special periods, criticism can only regard it as by some kind of miracle that the humane life exists at all among us, or that our cultural prospects are even as cheerful as they are.

II

For the humane life does exist among us, and as far as one person's observation goes, it reaches a higher individual development all round among us than in any other society I know of. The reason why our cultural prospects are so poor is not, as is sometimes very superficially said, that there is no culture here. On the contrary, the best culture that I have ever seen, judged by its fruits—culture taking shape in lucidity of mind, intellectual curiosity and hospitality, largeness of temper, objectivity, the finest sense of social life, of manners, of beauty—was in the United States. The aggregate of it is much less, relatively. than elsewhere; but scanty, frail, and unproductive as it is, I have never seen better.

75

Nor is there any more value in the equally superficial observation that Americans do not much care for culture. What people, left to their own devices and preferences, ever did much care for culture? The general diffusion and prevalence of culture, as far as it has gone, has always been an effect of the high culture of certain classes. In Europe, where people care more for culture than we do, one cannot help observing how largely the love of it is traditional, and how much of the technical apparatus of culture, on which their own culture is patterned, and by which their love of culture is both stimulated and regulated—how much of all this has come to them by way of sheer legacy. Take out the cultural vestiges and traditions of about three royal courts, and anyone travelling through France can easily reckon the mighty shrinkage of French cultural apparatus and the slowing-down of the general tradition's momentum. The approach to culture is laborious and discouraging, and the natural man dislikes work and is easily discouraged. Spiritual activity is too new a thing in the experience of the race; men have not been at it long enough to be at ease in it. It is like the upright position; men can and do assume the upright position, but seldom keep to it longer than necessary—they sit down when they can. The majority have always preferred an inferior good that was more easily acquired and more nearly immediate, unless they were subjected to some strong stimulus which for collateral reasons made the sacrifices demanded by culture seem worth while. Matthew Arnold quotes the learned Martinus Scriblerus's saying (being far from books at the moment, I must quote from memory) that the taste for the bathos is implanted by nature deep in the soul of man, and that it governs him "until, perverted by custom or example, he is brought, or rather compelled, to relish the sublime."

The Church in the Middle Ages could, and did, exercise this power of perversion. It never has had half enough credit for the cultural effect of what it did, even though, for reasons of its own, it did not do all it might have done. The royal courts could exercise the same power, and many of them did, like that of Francis I, for example, and some of the Bavarian kings. Sometimes they coöperated with the Church, thus directing two powerful forces towards the same end. The Church and the court were in a position, not only to organize spiritual activity of various kinds, but also to give it a prestige that made effective headway against the natural taste for the bathos. With these assistances and recommendations, culture got over its initial obstacles, and later could make its own way, relying upon its own power of attraction. The Belgians were always a musical people after their own fashion, and a very good and interesting fashion, but the Elector of Bavaria, Max-Emmanuel, when Governor of the Netherlands, organized music as a function of the civil service, thus giving it a prestige whereby the Belgians were brought "to relish the sublime" in that art, as they still do, and would probably for some time continue to do, even if the royal patronage of music were withdrawn. It is not generally understood, I think, that a very extensive organization of spiritual activity once took place on our continent, in the Mormon polity under Brigham Young; and though it remained in force so short a time, traces of its effect are still plainly to be seen.

Now, it is the lack in America of any influence that by common consent can exercise just

this power of perversion, which makes the out-
look for culture so unpromising. The person
who looks wistfully at culture must go forward
practically alone against the full force of wind
and tide. Such culture as we have is solitary
and uninfluential, existing fortuitously, like
stonecrop in the interstices of a much-trodden
pavement. One can imagine nothing more dis-
regarded, disparaged, more out of the general
run of American affairs. By general consent
culture has no place in our institutional life;
not in the pulpit, not in the public service or
in journalism, notoriously not in our colleges
and schools, not in our literature—such of our
literature, at least, with rare and very interesting exceptions, as gets itself easily published
and considerably read. Here again, however,
criticism, while regretting the fact, can see
nothing unnatural in it, and nothing susceptible
of immediate change. Our whole institutional
life is carried on with a view to objects and
purposes which are not those of culture; and
the complete alienation of culture from its
processes is, therefore, quite to be expected. It
is simply a fact to be remarked, not a condition
to be complained of. In other civilizations the

natural taste for the bathos has been, by common consent, severely modified through processes of perversion; but in ours it has been glorified, by common consent, into unapproachable dominance.

To the eye of criticism, some of the consequences of this are interesting. With the natural taste for the bathos everywhere unrestrained and rampant, there is hardly anyone among us who suspects the existence of impersonal critical standards, much less feels it incumbent on him to pay them any respect. A European would see at once, for instance, why a ruler like Frederick the Great, whose position raised him above pettiness and self-interest, with advisers like von Humboldt and Schleiermacher, would be likely to devise a better system of secondary schools than could be worked out by some local school-board appointed by a mayor. An American would not see it so easily; ten to one he would say the local board would do better, as more likely "to give the people what they want"—more likely, that is, to meet the grand average of local taste for the bathos. Thus, there really exists no sense among us of what is first class, second class, third or fourth class, or of what makes it so. Everyone has noticed that our reviewers bestow exactly the same order of praise on a fourth-class work of art—a book, for example—that they do upon a first-class work. I have now before me, for instance, some reviews of a new novel; and two or three of the writers—men of some pretensions, whose word goes a long way with readers, I understand—could not be more earnestly reverential if they were speaking of Cervantes's masterpiece. I have not read the novel, and it may be very great, of course, but really can it be *that* great? With all my best wishes for the author, I fear not. Many fourth-class books indeed deserve high praise; we all have read such books with pleasure, and with no less pleasure because we knew all the time that they were fourth-class books, and knew why they were such, and knew that the pleasure we were getting out of them was of an entirely different order from that which we get out of first-class books. A fourth-class book is not *ipso facto* to be disparaged, for it may be very good indeed; but neither is it to be spoken of in the same terms that one would use of a first-class book, and no writer with any critical sense—

no writer, that is, who was depending on something above and beyond a mere personal estimate of the work before him—would dream of doing so.

In this general critical insensitiveness, Americans remind one of those large worms of the species called Eunice, I think, which will begin to eat their own bodies if they discover them lying in range of their mouth. Americans have no Philistine objection to a good thing; on the contrary, they often accept it. But they accept it without exercising any critical faculty upon it; without really knowing that it is good, or knowing what makes it so. Their estimate is purely personal. Until this is understood it seems anomalous, for example, that a work like that of Professor Adams should be a best-seller, as for some time it was. But they will also accept a bad thing with equal interest and with the same critical insensitiveness, especially if it bears some kind of specious recommendation. At the Opéra-Comique, not long ago, I sat beside a very civil and pleasant stranger who turned out to be an American, through all that I could endure of the very worst performance of "Hoffmann" I ever heard in my life. After the first act my neighbour praised it with immense enthusiasm, which embarrassed me into silence. Finally, however, being obliged to say something, I said that, having heard the same opera so lately at Brussels, I supposed I was rather spoiled. "Ah, Brussels!" he said. "Well, now, that's interesting. I overheard somebody saying that same thing out in the street, just as I was coming in. But I didn't pay much attention to it, you know, because I sort of took for granted that the best performances must be here in Paris."

It would be unfair to press this illustration too far, because very few Americans nowadays, especially if they live in New York, have a chance to hear even a tolerable performance of "Hoffmann." But without any unfairness, the reader will have no trouble in getting the implication. A visiting European would have been likely to know that the performance we heard was bad; he would have known why it was bad; and the fact of its being given at the Opéra-Comique in Paris would have had no weight with him whatever. The great majority of Americans (without prejudice to the gentleman who sat beside me) are quite devoid of

83

this critical faculty. What they encounter under some special set of altogether unrelated circumstances they are predisposed to accept and applaud, quite unaware that there is a strict impersonal standard set for such matters, and that, according to this standard, the thing they are accepting may be rated very low indeed. This uncritical attitude appears in every department of spiritual activity, and indulgence in it is unchecked by any organized influence of any kind.

Indeed, every organized influence is actively on the other side; it is on the side of the cultural taste for the bathos. When Francis I or the Elector Max-Emmanuel or Richelieu set out to make some partial and indirect recommendation of the humane life—to show in some measure what a good, desirable, and satisfactory thing it is—he had a fairly clear field. He did not find the natural taste for the bathos immensely fortified by innumerable mechanical accessories, and flattered by all the arts of salesmanship employed in disposing of them. This is the crucial difference, from the standpoint of culture, that criticism observes between the times, say, of the Elector Max and those of

Albert I. When the Elector Max established the Monnaie, he had hardly any competition to meet. There was no horde of commercial enterprisers busily encouraging the popular taste for the bathos to believe that it was good taste, just as good as anybody's, that its standards were all right, and that all it had to do was to keep on its natural way in order to come out as well as need be, and to realize as complete satisfaction as the human spirit demands. This is the kind of thing which Albert I, in continuing the Elector Max's tradition, has to meet; and in America where there has never been any authoritative tradition, and no power capable of establishing one, this is the kind of thing which goes on in greater strength and larger extension than anywhere else in the world.

III

This is the condition that really determines the forecast which criticism is obliged to make for culture in America. The situation, viewed *in limine*, is clearly quite hopeless; and criticism makes this forecast, I repeat, without blame, and, as I shall show presently, without despair or depression. What is the use of recommend-

ing the satisfactions of spiritual activity to people who are already quite satisfied amid the in-
conceivable multiplicity of mechanical accessories and organized promotions of spiritual
inactivity?   Tell them, as our prophets and
reformers do, that the natural taste for the
bathos is educable and improvable, and that they
ought to do something about it in order to attain the highest degree of happiness possible
to humanity, and they reply, "You may be right,
but we are not interested.   We are doing quite
well as we are.   Spiritual activity is hard work;
nobody else is doing it, and we are getting on
comfortably without any work.   We have plenty
of distractions to take up our time, plenty of
good company, everybody is going our way and
nobody going yours."   What can one answer?
Nothing, simply—there is no answer.

There never was a time of so many and so
powerful competitive distractions contesting
with culture for the employment of one's hours,
and directly tending towards the reinforcement
and further degradation of the natural taste
for the bathos.   One has but to think of the
enormous army of commercial enterprisers engaged in pandering to this taste and employ-

ing every conceivable device of ingenuity to confirm and flatter and reassure it. Publishers, newspaper-proprietors, editors, preachers, purveyors of commercial amusement, college presidents—the list is endless—all aim consciously at the lowest common denominator of public intelligence, taste, and character. One may not say that they do this willingly in all cases, but they do it consciously. But this is not all. Usually for social reasons or, one may say, for purposes of exhibition, the natural taste for bathos still largely pays a kind of acknowledgement to the superiority of culture. This acknowledgment takes the form of a willingness, or even a desire, to assume the appearance of culture and counterfeit its superficial qualities. Commercial enterprise has seized upon this disposition and made as much of it as it can, thereby administering to the natural taste for the bathos the subtlest flattery of all. Thus in literature, education, music, art, in every department of spiritual activity, we have developed an impressive system of passive exercise in culture, a system proposing to produce a sound natural development while the mind of the patient remains completely and comfortably inert upon

87

its native plane of thought and imagination. The apparatus of this substitutionary process is well known to everyone; the "outline" of this or that, the travel bureau, the lecture bureau, the Browning club, the Joseph Conrad club, and so on. Its peak of organization, by the testimony of William James, is reached at Chautauqua. Thus the pursuit of an imitation or Brummagem culture is industriously sophisticated by brisk young college professors with an agreeable gift for miscellaneous volubility, and effeminized by the patronage of women's clubs. I have every wish that this last observation shall not be misunderstood. Whatever may have been the case at the beginning, I feel sure that if the work and influence of women were now subtracted from our society we should after a short time have very little of a civilized environment left. The cartoonist's count against the male of the species, I think, is a true one—I know it is true against myself—that, left to his own devices, he contentedly lapses into squalor. All I suggest is that the natural taste for the bathos knows no distinction of sex. The uncritical attitude towards affairs of the spirit is common to women and

88

men. Among us, spiritual activity, or the counterfeit of it, has always been popularly regarded
as lying quite exclusively in woman's province;
indeed, our economic system has already brought
men pretty well down to the anthropoid level
by condemning them to incessant preoccupation
with the mere means of existence. Hence our
apparatus of culture and our management of it
are peculiarly susceptible to the feminine variant of the natural taste for the bathos. Perhaps
one sees a fair example of this susceptibility, and
the fruits of it, in our development of music,
with its relatively great interest in the personality of artists, and its slight interest in the pro-
grammes that the artists execute.

It must never be forgotten—one cannot be
insisting on it at every paragraph in an essay
of this length—that culture has not for its final
object the development of intelligence and taste,
but the profound transformations of character
that can only be effected by the self-imposed
discipline of culture. An appearance of culture,
effected by no discipline whatever, but only by
docility in following one's nose, cannot bring
about these transformations. It is not to be
doubted, I think, that Americans will soon have

89

a very considerable nodding acquaintance with the best in literature and in the other arts, which is the working apparatus of culture; many influences, mostly commercial, already conspire to promote this. But the transformations of character, which are the only fruit of culture that make it worth serious recommendation, are not to be brought about in that way. It is one thing, for the sake of collateral purposes unrelated to culture, to desire this nodding acquaintance and to undergo the passive exercise necessary to get it; and it is quite another thing to desire the transformations of character attainable only through culture, and to submit to the discipline of culture necessary to effect them.

Probably everyone who is more or less occupied in the works and ways of culture runs across an occasional spirit, usually young and ardent, who desires the fruits of culture and welcomes the discipline that brings them forth. Sanguine persons argue from this phenomenon that matters look brighter, bidding us think of what the grandparents of these young people, and the society that surrounded them, were like. Criticism, however, measures the strength of the opposite pull on these young people of the present day, discriminates carefully between real and apparent culture, as between leaves and fruit; it looks attentively into the matter of motive directed towards either, and it is obliged to regard this sign of promise as misleading. Superficially it is perhaps impressive, but actually it has little significance. I get letters from many such young spirits, and as so many come to an inconspicuous person like myself, I sometimes wonder how many come to persons whose relations with culture are in a sense official. I have two such letters this morning—what is one to say? The worst of it is that my correspondents mostly tell me they are not poor and that they have no responsibilities which would prevent their doing measurably what they like. Apparently they have enough in their favour; it is the imponderabilia that are against them. There is no trouble about telling them what to do, but one is all the time oppressed by the consciousness of delivering a counsel of perfection. How can one say to these correspondents, "Well, but the farther you progress in culture, the farther out of the current of affairs you put yourself, the more you are deprived of the

precious sense of coöperation with your fellows;
and this is a rather hard and forlorn prospect
for a young person to face"?   The author of
the *Imitation* said with great acuteness that "the
fewer there be who follow the way to heaven,
the harder that way is to find"—and, he might
have added, the harder to follow.   It is not to
be wondered at that these youthful spirits so
often abandon themselves to a sterile discontent,
and to a final weary acceptance of such slender
compromise as the iron force of the civilization
about them may yield.

Sanguine persons also get encouragement out
of the "revaluation-process" that they see, or
think they see, going on in America, and hope
for great things from it.   Criticism again, however, after taking stock of this process as benevo-
lently as it can, must regard their hopes as
illusory.   The pretended signs or symptoms of
revaluation mean actually nothing of the kind.
The present popularity of a certain type of historical and biographical writing, for instance,
argues nothing for culture.   It does not imply
any unusual energy of aspiration, or indeed
anything necessarily but a vagrant and vulgar
curiosity.   A very brief view of the most popu-

lar books of this type is enough to show this
clearly; one may see at a glance that their success is a success of scandal. So much may be
said for the type of social study presented in
pseudo-critical essays, and in the fiction produced
by what one of my friends describes as "cheeky
reporters with rather nasty minds." Criticism
does not pause to discuss the collateral effects
of this body of literature, but merely observes
that it does nothing for culture, and that any
expectations based upon its popularity had better
be given up. We all know that this literature
is almost invariably approached for the sake of
a kind of delectation which criticism must regard as extremely low. One approaches it to
have one's own vague malevolences, suspicions,
repugnances, formulated and confirmed, and
then reflected back upon one's own consciousness by force of a clever and specious style.
How many readers can one imagine approaching
Mr. Sinclair Lewis's novels, for instance, or
Mr. Mencken's essays in any other spirit than
that of Little Jack Horner? So far, then, from
tending towards the transformation of character
through culture, our whole body of "revalua-
tion-literature" really withstands and retards it.

93

Hence, too, the "revaluation-process," of which this literature is taken as symptomatic, appears to be greatly misapprehended; and this misapprehension, again, assists in the sacrifice of one generation at least, and, for all that can now be seen to the contrary, of several.

IV

Criticism however, as I said, observes these untoward facts, observes even these lamentable sacrifices, without depression or despair. It is aware that culture and the humane life have one invincible ally on their side—the self-preserving instinct in humanity. This ally takes its time about asserting itself, but assert itself finally and effectively it always does. Ignorance, vulgarity, a barbaric and superficial spirit, may, and from all appearances will, predominate unquestioned for years in America, for ages if you like; no one can set a term on it. But a term there is, nevertheless, and when it is reached, men will come back to the quest of the humane life because they cannot do without it any longer. That is what has always happened, and it will happen again. Probably no one in that day will be able to tell just

what has moved them; the general currents
of life will simply reverse themselves and set
in the opposite direction, and no one will be
able to assign any better reason for it than that
humanity could not any longer put up with
their running the way they were. Perhaps by
that time the political entity which we now
know as the United States will have disappeared; one sees no reason to attach any peculiar permanence to it over any of the other
political entities that have come and gone.
Criticism, indeed, attaches very little importance to the bare question of the future of culture in the United States—*sub specie æternitatis,* what is the United States?   Criticism
knows well enough what the future of culture
will be, and it may tentatively observe that the
prospects in one place or another, for a few
generations or a few centuries perhaps, seem to
show this-or-that probable degree of correspondence with that future; but it interests itself no further. Virgil and Marcus Aurelius
had no nationalist conception of culture; anx-
iety about Roman culture was the last thing to
enter their minds. Socrates and his friends did
not inflate themselves with notions of the hu-

95

mane life as an Athenian property; they turned over all that kind of bombast to the politicians and publicists of the period, and threw in some rare humour for good measure, to keep it company. Their course is the one which criticism suggests as sincerely practical for Americans of the present time. Contemplating the future of culture in no set terms of nationality or race or time, they recognized the self-preserving instinct of mankind as on its side, and did not worry about it any further. On the contrary, they approached their own age with the understanding, equanimity, humour, and tolerance that culture indicates; and instead of expecting their civilization to give them more than it possibly could give them, instead of continually fretting at their fellow citizens, blaming, browbeating or expostulating with them for their derogations from the humane life, they bent their energies, as far as circumstances allowed, towards making some kind of progress in the humane life themselves.

Towards a New Quality-Product

I

*T*HERE are conventions, as well as tricks, in all trades. Every department of social activity being governed chiefly by convention, it is not surprising that the most powerful and far-reaching conventions are the least talked about. We know them, and obey them, but do not speak of them. In Gascony, probably, people do not talk much about gasconades, nor did the citizens of Gath have much to say about Philistinism. Thus the fundamental conventions that govern our American educational system are never discussed. Criticism and discussion are as a rule confined to matters of method; some of the superficial conventions are sometimes brought under fire; but the fundamental conventions are always left alone.

I propose to bring forward one or two of these conventions and discuss them, by way of preliminary to a practical suggestion. The first convention is that by which we tacitly assume that education and instruction are the same

97

thing, whereas they are really quite different. This is exactly comparable to the convention whereby we assume that republicanism, which is a political system under which everybody has a vote, is the same thing as democracy, which is primarily an economic status, and only secondarily political. Those who speak of the United States as a democracy, for instance, are misusing language most ludicrously, for it is no such thing, never was, and was never intended to be. The Fathers of the Republic were well aware of the difference between a republic and a democracy, and it is no credit to the intelligence of their descendents that the two are now almost invariably confused.

An instructional institution is not at all necessarily educational; whether it be actually so or not depends upon a variety of circumstances which are not usually reckoned with either in the professional or in the popular scale of speech. An instructed pupil is by no means necessarily an educated pupil, not even *in limine*; he is merely a person who has been exposed to instruction, with nothing implied about the effect of the exposure, which even from an instructional, let alone an educational, viewpoint, may quite well be no more than the effect of exposing a duck's back to rain. Whatever education accrues to him depends upon collateral circumstances and conditions. Therefore in speaking of instruction as equivalent to education, or *vice versa,* we misuse language. To avoid pedantry I shall keep on misusing it, for the purposes of this essay, except where the misuse would be ambiguous and perhaps misleading.

In earlier days this distinction was clearer. Ernest Renan long ago drew it with a firm hand, when he spoke of the United States as having set up "a considerable popular instruction without any serious higher education"—probably the most complete and competent criticism of our system that has ever been made, for all other general criticisms that I know of, and most of the special criticisms as well, are finally reducible to it. In the bad old times of the three R's and the deestrick school, the verb *to learn* had a transitive use, and in that use it was quite regularly pronounced *l'arn.* I am old enough to remember this, and hence old enough to mark the disappearance of the transitive form *to l'arn,* in favour of the active verb *to teach.* There seems to be a coincidence here, and a rather interesting one, because, as everyone knows who has tried it, you cannot teach a person anything—unless perchance he know it already—but you can l'arn him something. L'arnin' did not in those days, moreover, mean learning, as understood by us of the enlightened present; it did not mean the rather equivocal windfalls that drop in your path of passage from grade to grade of a course of instruction. Not even in its compound form *book-l'arnin'* did it mean precisely that. It meant something that somebody had l'arned you. I am not praising those old times, nor do I wish them back; I merely remark that a retrospect upon them discerns traces of this particular, and by no means useless or fantastic, discrimination.

A second fundamental convention that is never discussed is the one by which we assume that everybody ought to go to school. Some hardy educators lately have skirted the fringes of this convention by expressing doubt that everybody ought to go to college. The president of Brown University, in a recent interview, was quite outspoken about this. But as far as I know, no one has questioned the convention that regards all children as proper grist for the mill of the secondary schools. Our "compulsory education laws" as they are fancifully styled, embody this convention; so to question it would probably carry the implication of sedition as well as of heresy. Yet the "school age" which these laws specify counts for nothing, except conventionally; what really counts is school-ability; and the assumption that all children of school age have school-ability is flagrantly at variance with fact. If the law can do anything to encourage children of school-ability, irrespective of age, to go to school; if it can do anything to clear, illuminate, and beautify their path to school and through school, well and good. But the purely conventional content of these laws, in their present form, renders their practical application incompetent, fatuous, and vicious, and they ought to be remodeled in accordance with obvious fact and common sense. There was no need of the army tests to inform us that twelve million— or was it twenty?—of our younger people have not enough force of intellect to get them through the high school. Anyone casually considering a random assortment of our youngsters would be sure there are easily that many who are incapable of getting through any kind of secondary school with any profit whatever to themselves, to anyone else, or to the average of American citizenship.

All this seems extremely odd in view of our reputation for being a practical people. Education in the United States comes to a stupendous amount of money. Aside from public funds, the annual fees and disbursements to private secondary schools, colleges, universities, technical schools, are enormous. Having no statistics, I do not know how the gross sum compares with our annual outlay for chewing-gum, cosmetics, cigarettes, motor-cars, or contraband liquor; but one would be safe in saying that it is large enough to justify some sort of assurance about the kind of product that is being got for it. Yet just this is what no one seems able to give. No one seems to have even any very definite idea of the kind of product that is wanted, or any clear specifications for the kind that our system is attempting to produce.

II

It is probably the convergence of these two fundamental conventions upon the practical conduct of education that causes this uncertainty. Such uncertainty would at all events be the natural consequence of this convergence. Mr. Henry Ford is in no uncertainty about the kind of thing he wishes and intends to produce, or about the public demand for it; and he can give you a clear idea of the distinguishing points and qualities that his product will show when it comes out. This parallel cannot, of course, be pressed too far, because Mr. Ford is dealing with inanimate material, and our educational system is not. It may be usefully employed, however, to show the essential differences established by pure convention between production in Mr. Ford's case and in the case of our educational system.

Suppose there were a convention among the purchasing public which made them assume that aviation and motoring meant the same thing; one can easily imagine some of its reactions upon Mr. Ford in his capacity of manufacturer and salesman. When he met with his associates in the trade, for example, he would have to talk more or less in terms of aviation, and cudgel his brains for ways to keep these conventional trade-terms in some kind of far-fetched correspondence with the actualities of motoring. *Absurd!* some one will say. Quite so; but not an iota more absurd than the reactions set up by the inveterate conventional confusion of republicanism with democracy, or of education with instruction. To prove it, listen to any campaign speech or to any commencement address; or read a copy of the *Congressional Record,* or the proceedings of some gathering of pedagogues. If Mr. Henry Ford indulged in such inconsequent verbal antics before a group of his colleagues in the automobile industry, they would instantly adjourn as one man and apply for a commission *de lunatico inquirendo;* and they would be quite right.

One great reason, perhaps the greatest, why Mr. Ford can speak with such certainty about his product, is that he has control of his raw material and can keep it up to standard quality. Now suppose that, in addition to the convention already named, there were a strong social convention whereby everybody assumed that any kind of material, good, bad, or indifferent, would make up into a satisfactory motor-car; suppose, even, that there were a law compelling Mr. Ford, at certain seasons of the year, to accept and use all the culls that the American Tin Plate Company chose to shovel in on him in the course of its regular consignments. What forecast could Mr. Ford make of his product? None, obviously; one car might run ten thousand miles, the next one a hundred, and the next might not live to get out of the shop. For the same reason, largely, our educational system is utterly unable to give any more than a very meagre, vague, and prayerful account of the product that it can turn out.

Moreover, under these circumstances Mr. Ford could not even be much more explicit about the kind of product that he *intended* to turn out than about the kind he *expected* to turn out. If the poor man decided that the motor-car business were worth going on with at all, he would bend his harassed mind to the problem of modifying his processes in order to bring his product up as near as possible to the specifications set by these two insane conventions. He would remodel his factory to produce out of the average run of his material something which would have all the talking-points of a flying-machine that he could put into it, consistently with making it able to get over the ground in some fashion or other. If the material in one car were above the average, the product would be no worse than hybrid; it would not fly at all, its pretences in this direction being only a decorative folly, and it would not run on land as well as if it had been made in a factory where production was geared to standard material only.

Here we have a pretty fair parallel, again, to the plight of our educational system. Everybody ought to go to school; everybody ought to go to college. The worth and respectability of an educational institution is popularly measured by the size of its "plant" and the number of its students. A big school is a great school. Every institution, therefore, has to have students; it has to have regard to their numbers only, not their quality—anything that will make an additional name on the register will do, for social convention has decreed the assumption that everybody possesses school-ability. By due obeisance to this set of conventions and its corollaries, our institutions grew mightily until they reached their present proportions and their present scale of expense.

But it was soon found that everybody did not have school-ability of more than a rudimentary type, if even that. As the average of ability was watered down by the increased inflow of students, our educational system did just as we have supposed Mr. Ford might do under analogous conditions; it modified its processes so as to hit the least common denominator of ability in the material it dealt with. This modification was begun, as well as one can set a date to it, when the "elective system" was introduced at Harvard by the late President Eliot; who, in consequence, was enabled to ride the shoulders of American education like the Old Man of the Sea for nearly half a century, while the "elective system," which in principle is all very well for a university, made its way down into colleges and secondary schools—while, in short, education disappeared from among us, and instruction took its place. Before this period, as M. Renan said, America had indeed set up no serious higher education worth speaking of, but it had set up the beginnings, at least, of some

107

serious primary education, and of a little secondary education; it now may quite fairly be
said to have none of any kind. One should
say this, too, as I do, without complaint; for
what other measures of self-protection could
our system take in the face of the dominant
conventions? Executives like Mr. Butler and
Mr. Eliot (I hope his admirers will forgive me
for my plain speaking, for I too admire him
as much as they) are great interpreters of the
times; great educators, or, indeed, educators
of any degree, they are not and never could be,
and it is a disservice to them to obscure qualities worthy of all praise by a pretence that they
are.

Those who regard my parallel between our
educational system and Mr. Ford's enterprise
as extravagant and far-fetched, might give me
the benefit of a glance at the number and nature of the subjects taught in one representative
secondary school, college, and university—I
shall not suggest a choice, he may take his pick
—and an estimate of the amount of brain-fag
that an average mentality would suffer in "getting through" the minimum requirements laid
down to cover a judicious selection from the be-

wildering list. I think he would cheerfully exonerate me. Consider one item only, the "courses in English." Some time ago, in table talk with one of the most highly cultivated men in America, we tried to make a rough estimate of the number of "courses in English" that are offered annually by our colleges and universities. It came to something like twenty thousand, to my great amazement; and from my own observation and experience, which circumstances have made a little larger than the average, perhaps, I should say that these courses are the last refuge of the incompetent and the idle, though this is by no means the same as saying that no others ever take them. Forty years ago, I believe, a course in English was practically unknown among us; in the college I attended, back in the times of ignorance, such a thing was never dreamed of. Yet my fellow students managed somehow to write and speak pretty good English. On the other hand, I never yet had the pleasure of meeting a modern university graduate who had "specialized in English," who could either write English or speak English even tolerably. If my readers have had better luck, I congratulate them; I hope they have. Last year there fell under my hand a garland of literary windflowers culled from students by instructors, not in a primary school, not in a high school, not in a college, but in an American university, huge, prosperous, and flourishing. I do not know that the writers were "specializing in English"; but there they were, university students, and if one had not got one's eye-teeth cut, one might say they were therefore presumably literate, presumably intelligent. The following specimens bear testimony on these points:

"Being a tough hunk of meat, I passed up the steak."

"Lincoln's mind growed as his country kneaded it."

"The camel carries a water tank with him; he is also a rough rider and has four gates."

"As soon as music starts silence rains, but as soon as it stops it gets worse than ever."

"College students, as a general rule, like such readings that will take the least mental inertia."

"Modern dress is extreme and ought to be checked."

"Although the Irish are usually content with small jobs they have won a niche in the backbone of the country."

The instructor who reports these efforts also shows how Shakespeare fared at the hands of a group of sophomores and upper-classmen:

Edmund in "King Lear" "committed a base act and allowed his illegitimate father to see a forged letter." Cordelia's death "was the straw that broke the camel's back and killed the King." Lear's fool "was prostrated on the neck of the King." "Hotspur," averred a sophomore, "was a wild, irresolute man. He loved honor above all. He would go out and kill twenty Scotchmen before breakfast." Kate was a "woman who had something to do with hot spurs."

Also Milton:

"Diabetes was Milton's Italian friend," one student explained. Another said: "Satan had all the emotions of a woman and was a sort of trustee in heaven, so to speak." The theme of "Comus" was given as "purity protestriate." Mammon in "Paradise Lost" suggests that the best way "to endure hell is to raise hell and build a pavilion."

That will be about enough, I think. Let us ask ourselves once more what Mr. Ford would do in like premises, and then reverently take leave of the subject.

III

III

The third fundamental convention which besets our educational system is that by which we ignore the difference between formative knowledge and instrumental knowledge; the convention whereby we assume that instrumental knowledge is all one need have, that it will perfectly well do duty for formative knowledge; indeed, that it is in itself formative, as much so as any, and that the claims heretofore made for the formative power of another type of knowledge were hierarchical and spurious. When our system remodelled its processes to suit the requirements of educational mass-production (speaking in industrial terms) our educators began to talk a great deal about the need for our being "men of our time," and taking on only such studies as "adapt us to modern conditions" and "fit us to take our place in the present-day world"—such studies, in short, as directly bear on the business of becoming chemists, engineers, bond-salesmen, lawyers, horse-doctors, and so on. There was no direct relation superficially apparent between the type of study hitherto known as formative, and the ac-

112

tual practice of stock-jobbing, company-pro-
moting, or horse-doctoring; therefore this type
of study could and should be laid aside as a
sheer waste of time and effort. Time was a
great consideration, in fact, alike with students,
parents, and a public that, as Bishop Butler
says, was everywhere feverishly "impatient,
and for precipitating things." The public ideal
of excellence and success, generally speaking,
was embodied in men who had themselves never
been under the discipline of formative knowledge, and who neither wished nor were able to
appraise that discipline intelligently for others.
Our educational system at once rose to meet this
attitude of the public—what else could it do?—
and in the remodelling of its processes, formative studies either were flatly discarded or, when
they went on at all, went on only in a vestigial
fashion and under the blight of a general disregard and disparagement. At the present time
even, as well as I am informed, our system has
little or nothing to say about the relation of
formative knowledge to the vocational prac-
tices of a really educated citizenry. Yet there is
something to be said about it, and in view of
the state of our society, about which most

113

thoughtful observers have begun to be a little uneasy—a state resultant upon the unquestioned dominance of the conventions I have named— the subject seems worth reopening and reëxamining. President Butler of Columbia University was lately quoted by the newspapers as wondering why there are no longer any great men. The obvious rejoinder, of course, if one were ill-natured enough to make it, would be, How can there be any great men as long as Columbia University keeps on being what it is and doing what it does? The just rejoinder, however, is, How can there be any great men among us until the right relation between formative knowledge and instrumental knowledge becomes implicit in the actual practice and technique of education?

IV

While leading the world in mass-production, the United States also puts out a very slender and unconsidered line of quality-products that, as far as I know, are unequalled. The best suit of clothes I ever saw was made of an American homespun wool textile of which the entire annual output would not be enough, I dare say,

to keep Hart, Schaffner & Marx busy fifteen
minutes. Europe, the home of sausage, has
nothing that can hold a candle to the Kingston
sausage or the Lebanon County smoked sausage
of Pennsylvania. The best shaving-cream,
cologne-water, and mouth-wash I ever used
are American, made more or less for the fun
of the thing, apparently, by a very busy physician with a turn for chemistry, and if one can
ever get them, one is lucky; I do not believe
he takes time to make up a hundred dollars'
worth of all three together in a year, so he almost never has any of them on hand. The best
hard-water soap I ever saw—and, having an
uncommonly thin skin, I have diligently tried
many kinds, especially in our Lake regions, and
in Europe, where the water is as hard as
Pharaoh's heart—is American, made as a side
line by an old-time concern that does not seem
to care whether it sells any of it or not; and
hence the amount of search and supplication
necessary to get it would be enough, probably,
to reconcile a sinner to God, in a pinch. It is in
the *average* of such matters, and many others
that might be mentioned, that America ranks
relatively low; and it is, of course, by the

average that a country's production is to be judged. But the fact remains, as far as my experience goes, that in many lines America's quality-products, what little there is of them, and put out gingerly, almost surreptitiously, as they are, cannot be matched anywhere.

So it would seem that in a prosperous country of a hundred-odd million, where the mass-instructional system is wholly given over to the three conventions already cited, it might be possible to arouse some interest in a modest but very rigorous social experiment in quality-education, which should implacably defy those conventions. I have long had in mind a plan for such an experiment, in the shape of a strictly undergraduate college which should be limited to two hundred and fifty students. The only requirements for entrance should be (1) knowledge of arithmetic, and of algebra up to quadratics, (2) ability to read Greek and Latin, both prose and poetry, at sight, and to write Greek and Latin prose offhand. Nothing else, absolutely nothing, should be required, and any child worth educating can easily get up those requirements between the ages of eight and fifteen, if that is all he attempts to do. By read-

ing Greek and Latin at sight and writing them
offhand, I mean that when a boy entered this
college, all language-difficulties, all the mechanical work with vocabulary and structure,
should be forever behind him, and he should be
able to deal with Greek and Latin purely as
literature.

The curriculum of the college should cover
(1) the whole range of Greek and Roman literature, (2) mathematics up as far as the dif-
ferential calculus, (3) late in the course, six
or eight weeks work (three hours a week) in
formal logic; and still later, the same amount
of time on the *history* of the English language.
Nothing but that; the college should pursue
its mission as an educational experiment under
the most jealously safeguarded aseptic experimental conditions, and it should be understood
at the outset that the experiment could not be
expected to yield anything approximating con-
clusive data for at least fifty years.   There
should be no "student activities" of any kind.
The college should disallow and discourage any
quasi-official relations with its alumni, and dis-
countenance any representations from its alumni
concerning its administration.   When I went

117

to college, the authorities regarded the alumni as little better than the scum of the earth, and there would have been joy in the presence of the angels on the day that the alumni barged in with suggestions about how the place should be run, or with attempts to cultivate "college spirit," and induce undergraduates to do and die for their dear old *alma mater*. You may believe there would. My recollections of the general atmosphere of that institution are very vivid; it was an atmosphere untainted with sentimentalism of any kind. The students regarded the instructors as their natural enemies, hated them manfully, and respected them immeasureably. Anything like a specious and sentimental Elk-Rotarian good-fellowship between professor and student, in those days, was undreamed of; and the thought of it would have been as much resented by the students, on the score of propriety, as by the faculty. It has never yet been clear to me that this state of things was unwholesome or undesirable.

The college I have in mind should have its experimental status established in such economic security that it need not care twopence whether any students ever came to it or not, or think twice about bouncing its whole undergraduate body, if need be. In fact, if such a college were set up tomorrow, probably not a single student would enter it for the first six or seven years, and if it had a baker's dozen at the end of ten years, I should be surprised. After that, I should expect it very soon to reach a capacity attendance; and if it stood fifty years without graduating more than fifty men, I believe its character as a social experiment would have been vindicated.

The theory of this college would be that if a young man wanted to go into engineering or horse-doctoring or selling bonds, he might prepare for it after he had got through this inflexible course at the age of twenty-one or so, with the degree of B.A., the only degree that this college should be empowered to confer, and it would be a degree, by the way, that amply meant what it pretended to mean, instead of meaning nothing, as it now mostly does. The test of this theory would be made by some impartial track being kept of these graduates, to see not only how they compared in a vocational way with men of another type of training, but how they stood in all-round ability, enlightenment, character, general culture, general good judgment, and good sense; how their views of life, their demands on life and their discernment of its values, compared with those of their contemporaries otherwise trained.

V

For the purposes of this little essay I am not interested in trying to forecast the results of this test, or to show reasons for stipulating these educational terms for it, because I am not here propounding a thesis, but only making a suggestion. If the suggestion takes root with any one who might wish to endow such an experiment, I should be glad to go into the subject with him to any length and quite disinterestedly, as I have no sort of ax to grind. Almost the last thing I would choose to be at my time of life is a college president, or a professor, or *Gott soll hüten,* a trustee. My interest is only in a competent diagnosis of the weaknesses and disabilities of American civilization—disabilities which are every day increasingly apparent—and in finding some remedy for them; and I believe that the social experiment I have outlined would throw enough light on both these matters to be worth its cost. With our educational system continually controlled by the conventions which now control it (and there is no prospect that I can see of its release), our civilization is obviously likely to go on as it is. Argument *a priori* about the kind of civilization that might ensue upon an emancipation from these conventions would be as obviously futile and inert. Some line of practical approach, however, might be indicated *a posteriori,* by the experimental method, applied through such an institution as I have suggested; and in its essential features, as far as I am informed, there is not an institution in the United States today that remotely resembles the one I propose.

I discussed this idea at larger length lately with a young friend, a graduate of an English university, who wrote me as follows:

But think of the poor devils who will have gone through your mill! It seems a cold-blooded thing, merely by way of experiment, to turn out a lot of people who simply can't live at home. Vivisection is nothing to it. As I understand your scheme, you are planning to breed a batch of cultivated, sensitive beings who would all die six months after they were exposed to your actual civilization. This is not Oxford superciliousness, I assure you, for things nowadays are precious little better with us. I agree with you that such spirits are the salt of the earth, and England used to make some kind of place for them, not much, maybe, but there were back-waters where they could at least live and co-operate with their kind. But now—well, I hardly know. It seems as if some parts of the earth were jolly well salt-proof. The salt melts and disappears, and nothing comes of it.

This desponding sentiment may be sound or it may be unsound. But whatever one's opinion may be, I think that in spite of the chance of human sacrifice involved, an experiment tending towards something like actual evidence, one way or the other, would be greatly worth making.

Anarchist's Progress

I

*W*HEN I was seven years old, playing in front
of our house on the outskirts of Brooklyn one
morning, a policeman stopped and chatted with
me for a few moments. He was a kindly man,
of a Scandinavian blonde type with pleasant
blue eyes, and I took to him at once. He sealed
our acquaintance permanently by telling me a
story that I thought was immensely funny; I
laughed over it at intervals all day. I do not
remember what it was, but it had to do with
the antics of a drove of geese in our neighbourhood. He impressed me as the most entertaining and delightful person that I had seen in a
long time, and I spoke of him to my parents
with great pride.

At this time I did not know what policemen
were. No doubt I had seen them, but not to
notice them. Now, naturally, after meeting
this highly prepossessing specimen, I wished to
find out all I could about them, so I took the
matter up with our old colored cook. I learned

123

from her that my fine new friend represented
something that was called the law; that the
law was very good and great, and that everyone should obey and respect it. This was reasonable; if it were so, then my admirable friend
just fitted his place, and was even more highly
to be thought of, if possible. I asked where
the law came from, and it was explained to me
that men all over the country got together on
what was called election day, and chose certain
persons to make the law and others to see that it
was carried out; and that the sum-total of all
this mechanism was called our government.
This again was as it should be; the men I
knew, such as my father, my uncle George, and
Messrs. So-and-so among the neighbours (running them over rapidly in my mind), could do
this sort of thing handsomely, and there was
probably a good deal in the idea. But what
was it all for? Why did we have law and
government, anyway? Then I learned that
there were persons called criminals; some of
them stole, some hurt or killed people or set
fire to houses; and it was the duty of men like
my friend the policeman to protect us from
them. If he saw any he would catch them and

lock them up, and they would be punished according to the law.

A year or so later we moved to another house in the same neighbourhood, only a short distance away. On the corner of the block—rather a long block—behind our house stood a large one-story wooden building, very dirty and shabby, called the Wigwam. While getting the lie of my new surroundings, I considered this structure and remarked with disfavour the kind of people who seemed to be making themselves at home there. Some one told me it was a "political headquarters," but I did not know what that meant, and therefore did not connect it with my recent researches into law and government. I had little curiosity about the Wigwam. My parents never forbade my going there, but my mother once casually told me that it was a pretty good place to keep away from, and I agreed with her.

Two months later I heard some one say that election day was shortly coming on, and I sparked up at once; this, then, was the day when the lawmakers were to be chosen. There had been great doings at the Wigwam lately; in the evenings, too, I had seen noisy processions of drunken loafers passing our house, carrying transparencies, and tin torches that sent up clouds of kerosene-smoke. When I had asked what these meant, I was answered in one word, "politics," uttered in a disparaging tone, but this signified nothing to me. The fact is that my attention had been attracted by a steam-calliope that went along with one of the first of these processions, and I took it to mean that there was a circus going on; and when I found that there was no circus, I was disappointed and did not care what else might be taking place.

On hearing of election day, however, the light broke in on me. I was really witnessing the august performances that I had heard of from our cook. All these processions of yelling hoodlums who sweat and stank in the parboiling humidity of the Indian-summer evenings—all the squalid goings-on in the Wigwam—all these, it seemed, were part and parcel of an election. I noticed that the men whom I knew in the neighbourhood were not prominent in this election; my uncle George voted, I remember, and when he dropped in at our house that evening, I overheard him say that going to the polls was a filthy business. I could not

126

make it out.   Nothing could be clearer than
that the leading spirits in the whole affair were
most dreadful swine; and I wondered by what
kind of magic they could bring forth anything
so majestic, good and venerable as the law.
But I kept my questionings to myself for some
reason, though, as a rule, I was quite a hand
for pestering older people about matters that
seemed anomalous.   Finally, I gave it up as
hopeless, and thought no more about the subject for three years.

An incident of that election night, however,
stuck in my memory.   Some devoted brother,
very far gone in whisky, fell by the wayside in
a vacant lot just back of our house, on his way
to the Wigwam to await the returns.   He lay
there all night, mostly in a comatose state.   At
intervals of something like half an hour he
roused himself up in the darkness, apparently
aware that he was not doing his duty by the
occasion, and tried to sing the chorus of "March-
ing Through Georgia," but he could never get
quite through three measures of the first bar
before relapsing into somnolence.   It was very
funny; he always began so bravely and
earnestly, and always petered out so lamentably.

I often think of him. His general sense of political duty, I must say, still seems to me as intelligent and as competent as that of any man I have met in the many, many years that have gone by since then, and his mode of expressing it still seems about as effective as any I could suggest.

II

When I was just past my tenth birthday we left Brooklyn and went to live in a pleasant town of ten thousand population. An orphaned cousin made her home with us, a pretty girl, who soon began to cut a fair swath among the young men of the town. One of these was an extraordinary person, difficult to describe. My father, a great tease, at once detected his resemblance to a chimpanzee, and bored my cousin abominably by always speaking of him as Chim. The young man was not a popular idol by any means, yet no one thought badly of him. He was accepted everywhere as a source of legitimate diversion, and in the graduated, popular scale of local speech was invariably designated as a fool—a born fool, for which there was no help. When I heard he was a lawyer, I was

128

so astonished that I actually went into the chicken-court one day to hear him plead some trifling case, out of sheer curiosity to see him in action; and I must say I got my money's worth. Presently the word went around that he was going to run for Congress, and stood a good chance of being elected; and what amazed me above all was that no one seemed to see anything out of the way about it.

My tottering faith in law and government got a hard jolt from this. Here was a man, a very good fellow indeed—he had nothing in common with the crew who herded around the Wigwam—who was regarded by the unanimous judgment of the community, without doubt, peradventure, or exception, as having barely sense enough to come in when it rained; and this was the man whom his party was sending to Washington as contentedly as if he were some Draco or Solon. At this point my sense of humour forged to the front and took permanent charge of the situation, which was fortunate for me, since otherwise my education would have been aborted, and I would perhaps, like so many who have missed this great blessing, have gone in with the reformers and uplifters; and such a close shave as this, in the words of Rabelais, is a terrible thing to think upon. How many reformers there have been in my day; how nobly and absurdly busy they were, and how dismally unhumorous! I can dimly remember Pingree and Altgeld in the Middle West, and Godkin, Strong, and Seth Low in New York. During the 'nineties, the goodly fellowship of the prophets buzzed about the whole country like flies around a tar-barrel —and, Lord! where be they now?

III

It will easily be seen, I think, that the only unusual thing about all this was that my mind was perfectly unprepossessed and blank throughout. My experiences were surely not uncommon, and my reasonings and inferences were no more than any child, who was more than half-witted, could have made without trouble. But my mind had never been perverted or sophisticated; it was left to itself. I never went to school, so I was never indoctrinated with pseudo-patriotic fustian of any kind, and the plain, natural truth of such matters as I have been describing, therefore, found its way to my mind without encountering any artificial obstacle.

This freedom continued, happily, until my mind had matured and toughened. When I went to college I had the great good luck to hit on probably the only one in the country (there certainly is none now) where all such subjects were so remote and unconsidered that one would not know they existed. I had Greek, Latin, and mathematics, and nothing else, but I had these until the cows came home; then I had them all over again (or so it seemed) to make sure nothing was left out; then I was given a bachelor's degree in the liberal arts, and turned adrift. The idea was that if one wished to go in for some special branch of learning, one should do it afterward, on the foundation laid at college. The college's business was to lay the foundation, and the authorities saw to it that we were kept plentifully busy with the job. Therefore, all such subjects as political history, political science, and political economy were closed to me throughout my youth and early manhood; and when the time came that I wished to look into them, I did it on my own, without the interference of instructors, as any

131

person who has gone through a course of training similar to mine at college is quite competent
to do.

That time, however, came much later, and
meanwhile I thought little about law and government, as I had other fish to fry; I was living
more or less out of the world, occupied with
literary studies. Occasionally some incident
happened that set my mind perhaps a little farther along in the old sequences, but not often.
Once, I remember, I ran across the case of a
boy who had been sentenced to prison, a poor,
scared little brat, who had intended something
no worse than mischief, and it turned out to be
a crime. The judge said he disliked to sentence
the lad; it seemed the wrong thing to do; but
the law left him no option. I was struck by
this. The judge, then, was doing something
as an official that he would not dream of doing
as a man; and he could do it without any sense
of responsibility, or discomfort, simply because
he was acting as an official and not as a man.
On this principle of action, it seemed to me
that one could commit almost any kind of crime
without getting into trouble with one's conscience. Clearly, a great crime had been com-

mitted against this boy; yet nobody who had had a hand in it—the judge, the jury, the prosecutor, the complaining witness, the policemen and jailers—felt any responsibility about it, because they were not acting as men, but as officials. Clearly, too, the public did not regard them as criminals, but rather as upright and conscientious men.

The idea came to me then, vaguely but unmistakably, that if the primary intention of government was not to abolish crime but merely to monopolize crime, no better device could be found for doing it than the inculcation of precisely this frame of mind in the officials and in the public; for the effect of this was to exempt both from any allegiance to those sanctions of humanity or decency which anyone of either class, acting as an individual, would have felt himself bound to respect—nay, would have wished to respect. This idea was vague at the moment, as I say, and I did not work it out for some years, but I think I never quite lost track of it from that time.

Presently I got acquainted in a casual way with some officeholders, becoming quite friendly with one in particular, who held a high elective office. One day he happened to ask me how I would reply to a letter that bothered him; it was a query about the fitness of a certain man for an appointive job. His recommendation would have weight; he liked the man, and really wanted to recommend him—moreover, he was under great political pressure to recommend him—but he did not think the man was qualified. Well, then, I suggested offhand, why not put it just that way?—it seemed all fair and straightforward. "Ah yes," he said, "but if I wrote such a letter as that, you see, I wouldn't be reëlected." This took me aback a bit, and I demurred somewhat. "That's all very well," he kept insisting, "but I wouldn't be reëlected." Thinking to give the discussion a semi-humorous turn, I told him that the public, after all, had rights in the matter; he was their hired servant, and if he were not reelected it would mean merely that the public did not want him to work for them any more, which was quite within their competence. Moreover, if they threw him out on any such issue as this, he ought to take it as a compliment; indeed, if he were reëlected, would it not tend to show in some measure that he and the people

did not fully understand each other? He did
not like my tone of levity, and dismissed the
subject with the remark that I knew nothing
of practical politics, which was no doubt true.

IV

Perhaps a year after this I had my first view
of a legislative body in action. I visited the
capital of a certain country, and listened attentively to the legislative proceedings. What I
wished to observe, first of all, was the kind
of business that was mostly under discussion;
and next, I wished to get as good a general idea
as I could of the kind of men who were en-
trusted with this business. I had a friend on
the spot, formerly a newspaper reporter who
had been in the press gallery for years; he
guided me over the government buildings, taking me everywhere and showing me everything
I asked to see.

As we walked through some corridors in the
basement of the Capitol, I remarked the reso-
nance of the stonework. "Yes," he said,
thoughtfully, "these walls, in their time, have
echoed to the uncertain footsteps of many a
drunken statesman." His words were made good

in a few moments when we heard a spirited com-
motion ahead, which we found to proceed from a
good-sized room, perhaps a committee room,
opening off the corridor. The door being open,
we stopped, and looked in on a strange sight.

In the centre of the room, a florid, square-
built, portly man was dancing an extraordinary
kind of break-down, or *kazák* dance. He leaped
straight up to an incredible height, spun around
like a teetotum, stamped his feet, then suddenly
squatted and hopped through several measures
in a squatting position, his hands on his knees,
and then leaped up in the air and spun around
again. He blew like a turkey-cock, and occasionally uttered hoarse cries; his protruding and
fiery eyes were suffused with blood, and the
veins stood out on his neck and forehead like
the strings of a bass-viol. He was drunk.

About a dozen others, also very drunk, stood
around him in crouching postures, some clap-
ping their hands and some slapping their knees,
keeping time to the dance. One of them
caught sight of us in the doorway, came up, and
began to talk to me in a maundering fashion
about his constituents. He was a loathsome human being; I have seldom seen one so repulsive.

136

I could make nothing of what he said; he was almost inarticulate; and in pronouncing certain syllables he would slaver and spit, so that I was more occupied with keeping out of his range than with listening to him. He kept trying to buttonhole me, and I kept moving backward; he had backed me thirty feet down the corridor when my friend came along and disengaged me; and as we resumed our way, my friend observed for my consolation that "you pretty well need a mackintosh when X talks to you, even when he is sober."

This man, I learned, was interested in the looting of certain valuable public lands; nobody had heard of his ever being interested in any other legislative measures. The florid man who was dancing was interested in nothing but a high tariff on certain manufactures; he shortly became a Cabinet officer. Throughout my stay I was struck by seeing how much of the real business of legislation was in this category— how much, that is, had to do with putting unearned money in the pockets of beneficiaries— and what fitful and perfunctory attention the legislators gave to any other kind of business. I was even more impressed by the prevalent air

of cynicism; by the frankness with which everyone seemed to acquiesce in the view of Voltaire,
that government is merely a device for taking
money out of one person's pocket and putting
it into another's.

V

These experiences, commonplace as they
were, prepared me to pause over and question
certain sayings of famous men, when subse-
quently I ran across them, which otherwise I
would perhaps have passed by without thinking about them. When I came upon the saying
of Lincoln, that the way of the politician is
"a long step removed from common honesty,"
it set a problem for me. I wondered just why
this should be generally true, if it were true.
When I read the remark of Mr. Jefferson, that
"whenever a man has cast a longing eye on office, a rottenness begins in his conduct," I remembered the judge who had sentenced the
boy, and my officeholding acquaintance who was
so worried about reëlection. I tried to re-
examine their position, as far as possible putting
myself in their place, and made a great effort

138

to understand it favorably. My first view of a parliamentary body came back to me vividly when I read the despondent observation of John Bright, that he had sometimes known the British Parliament to do a good thing, but never just because it was a good thing. In the meantime I had observed many legislatures, and their principal occupations and preoccupations seemed to me precisely like those of the first one I ever saw; and while their personnel was not by any means composed throughout of noisy and disgusting scoundrels (neither, I· hasten to say, was the first one), it was so unimaginably inept that it would really have to be seen to be believed. I cannot think of a more powerful stimulus to one's intellectual curiosity, for instance, than to sit in the galleries of the last Congress, contemplate its general run of membership, and then recall these sayings of Lincoln, Mr. Jefferson, and John Bright.[1]

[1] As indicating the impression made on a more sophisticated mind, I may mention an amusing incident that happened to me in London two years ago. Having an engagement with a member of the House of Commons, I filled out a card and gave it to an attendant. By mistake I had written my name where the member's should be, and his where mine should be. The attendant handed the card

It struck me as strange that these phenomena seemed never to stir any intellectual curiosity in anybody. As far as I know, there is no record of its ever having occurred to Lincoln that the fact he had remarked was striking enough to need accounting for; nor yet to Mr. Jefferson, whose intellectual curiosity was almost boundless; nor yet to John Bright. As for the people around me, their attitudes seemed strangest of all. They all disparaged politics. Their common saying, "Oh, that's politics," always pointed to something that in any other sphere of action they would call shabby and disreputable. But they never asked themselves why it was that in this one sphere of action alone they took shabby and disreputable conduct as a matter of course. It was all the more strange because these same people still somehow assumed that politics existed for the promotion of the highest social purposes. They assumed that the State's primary purpose was to promote through appropriate institutions the general welfare of its members. This assump-

back, saying, "I'm afraid this will 'ardly do, sir. I see you've been making yourself a member. It doesn't go quite as easy as that, sir—though from some of what you see around 'ere, I wouldn't say as 'ow you mightn't think so."

tion, whatever it amounted to, furnished the
rationale of their patriotism, and they held to it
with a tenacity that on slight provocation became vindictive and fanatical. Yet all of them
were aware, and if pressed, could not help ac-
knowledging, that more than 90 per cent of the
State's energy was employed directly against
the general welfare. Thus one might say that
they seemed to have one set of credenda for
week-days and another for Sundays, and never
to ask themselves what actual reasons they had
for holding either.

I did not know how to take this, nor do I
now. Let me draw a rough parallel. Suppose
vast numbers of people to be contemplating a
machine that they had been told was a plough,
and very valuable—indeed, that they could not
get on without it—some even saying that its
design came down in some way from on high.
They have great feelings of pride and jealousy
about this machine, and will give up their lives
for it if they are told it is in danger. Yet they
all see that it will not plough well, no matter
what hands are put to manage it, and in fact
does hardly any ploughing at all; sometimes
only, with enormous difficulty and continual

141

tinkering and adjustment can it be got to scratch
a sort of furrow, very poor and short, hardly
practicable, and ludicrously disproportionate to
the cost and pains of cutting it. On the other
hand, the machine harrows perfectly, almost
automatically. It looks like a harrow, has the
history of a harrow, and even when the most
enlightened effort is expended on it to make
it act like a plough, it persists, except for an
occasional six or eight per cent of efficiency, in
acting like a harrow.

Surely such a spectacle would make an intelligent being raise some enquiry about the
nature and original intention of that machine.
Was it really a plough? Was it ever meant to
plough with? Was it not designed and constructed for harrowing? Yet none of the
anomalies that I had been observing ever raised
any enquiry about the nature and original intention of the State. They were merely acquiesced
in. At most, they were put down feebly to the
imperfections of human nature which render
mismanagement and perversion of every good
institution to some extent inevitable; and this is
absurd, for these anomalies do not appear in
the conduct of any other human institution. It

is no matter of opinion, but of open and notorious fact, that they do not. There are anomalies in the church and in the family that are significantly analogous; they will bear investigation, and are getting it; but the analogies are by no means complete, and are mostly due to the historical connection of these two institutions with the State.

Everyone knows that the State claims and exercises the monopoly of crime that I spoke of a moment ago, and that it makes this monopoly as strict as it can. It forbids private murder, but itself organizes murder on a colossal scale. It punishes private theft, but itself lays unscrupulous hands on anything it wants, whether the property of citizen or of alien. There is, for example, no human right, natural or Constitutional, that we have not seen nullified by the United States Government. Of all the crimes that are committed for gain or revenge, there is not one that we have not seen it commit—murder, mayhem, arson, robbery, fraud, criminal collusion and connivance. On the other hand, we have all remarked the enormous relative difficulty of getting the State to effect any measure for the general welfare. Compare the difficulty of securing conviction in cases of notorious malfeasance, and in cases of petty private crime. Compare the smooth and easy going of the Teapot Dome transactions with the obstructionist behaviour of the State toward a national child-labour law. Suppose one should try to get the State to put the same safeguards (no stronger) around service-income that with no pressure at all it puts around capital-income: what chance would one have? It must not be understood that I bring these matters forward to complain of them. I am not concerned with complaints or reforms, but only with the exhibition of anomalies that seem to me to need accounting for.

VI

In the course of some desultory reading I noticed that the historian Parkman, at the outset of his volume on the conspiracy of Pontiac, dwells with some puzzlement, apparently, upon the fact that the Indians had not formed a State. Mr. Jefferson, also, who knew the Indians well, remarked the same fact—that they lived in a rather highly organized society, but had never formed a State. Bicknell, the his-

144

torian of Rhode Island, has some interesting
passages that bear upon the same point, hinting
that the collisions between the Indians and the
whites may have been largely due to a misun-
derstanding about the nature of land-tenure;
that the Indians, knowing nothing of the British system of land-tenure, understood their
land-sales and land-grants as merely an admis-
sion of the whites to the same communal use of
land that they themselves enjoyed. I noticed,
too, that Marx devotes a good deal of space in
Das Kapital to proving that economic exploitation cannot take place in any society until the
exploited class has been expropriated from the
land. These observations attracted my attention as possibly throwing a strong side light
upon the nature of the State and the primary
purpose of government, and I made note of
them accordingly.

At this time I was a good deal in Europe. I
was in England and Germany during the
Tangier incident, studying the circumstances
and conditions that led up to the late war. My
facilities for this were exceptional, and I used
them diligently. Here I saw the State behav-
ing just as I had seen it behave at home. More-

over, remembering the political theories of the
eighteenth century, and the expectations put
upon them, I was struck with the fact that the
republican, constitutional-monarchical and auto-
cratic States behaved exactly alike.   This has
never been sufficiently remarked.   There was
no practical distinction to be drawn among England, France, Germany, and Russia; in all these
countries the State acted with unvarying con-
sistency and unfailing regularity against the interests of the immense, the overwhelming majority of its people.   So flagrant and flagitious,
indeed, was the action of the State in all these
countries, that its administrative officials, especially its diplomats, would immediately, in any
other sphere of action, be put down as a profes-
sional-criminal class; just as would the corresponding officials in my own country, as I had
already remarked.   It is a noteworthy fact, indeed, concerning all that has happened since
then, that if in any given circumstances one
went on the assumption that they were a pro-
fessional-criminal class, one could predict with
accuracy what they would do and what would
happen; while on any other assumption one

could predict almost nothing. The accuracy of my own predictions during the war and throughout the Peace Conference was due to nothing but their being based on this assumption.

The Liberal party was in power in England in 1911, and my attention became attracted to its tenets. I had already seen something of Liberalism in America as a kind of glorified mugwumpery. The Cleveland Administration had long before proved what everybody already knew, that there was no essential difference between the Republican and Democratic parties; an election meant merely that one was in office and wished to stay in, and the other was out and wished to get in. I saw precisely the same relation prevailing between the two major parties in England, and I was to see later the same relation sustained by the Labour Administration of Mr. Ramsay MacDonald. All these political permutations resulted only in what John Adams admirably called "a change of impostors." But I was chiefly interested in the basic theory of Liberalism. This seemed to be that the State is no worse than a degenerate or perverted institution, beneficent in its original

147

intention, and susceptible of restoration by the simple expedient of "putting good men in office."

I had already seen this experiment tried on several scales of magnitude, and observed that it came to nothing commensurate with the expectations put upon it or the enormous difficulty of arranging it. Later I was to see it tried on an unprecedented scale, for almost all the Governments engaged in the war were Liberal, notably the English and our own. Its disastrous results in the case of the Wilson Administration are too well known to need comment; though I do not wish to escape the responsibility of saying that of all forms of political impostorship, Liberalism always seemed to me the most vicious, because the most pretentious and specious. The general upshot of my observations, however, was to show me that whether in the hands of Liberal or Conservative, Republican or Democrat, and whether under nominal constitutionalism, republicanism or autocracy, the mechanism of the State would work freely and naturally in but one direction, namely: against the general welfare of the people.

VII

So I set about finding out what I could about the origin of the State, to see whether its mechanism was ever really meant to work in any other direction; and here I came upon a very odd fact. All the current popular assumptions about the origin of the State rest upon sheer guesswork; none of them upon actual investigation. The treatises and textbooks that came into my hands were also based, finally, upon guesswork. Some authorities guessed that the State was originally formed by this-or-that mode of social agreement; others, by a kind of muddling empiricism; others, by the will of God; and so on. Apparently none of these, however, had taken the plain course of going back upon the record as far as possible to ascertain how it actually had been formed, and for what purpose. It seemed that enough information must be available; the formation of the State in America, for example, was a matter of relatively recent history, and one must be able to find out a great deal about it. Consequently I began to look around to see whether anyone had ever anywhere made any such investigation, and if so, what it amounted to.

I then discovered that the matter had, indeed, been investigated by scientific methods, and that all the scholars of the Continent knew about it, not as something new or startling, but as a sheer commonplace. The State did not originate in any form of social agreement, or with any disinterested view of promoting order and justice. Far otherwise. The State originated in conquest and confiscation, as a device for maintaining the stratification of society permanently into two classes—an owning and exploiting class, relatively small, and a propertyless dependent class. Such measures of order and justice as it established were incidental and ancillary to this purpose; it was not interested in any that did not serve this purpose; and it resisted the establishment of any that were contrary to it. No State known to history originated in any other manner, or for any other purpose than to enable the continuous economic exploitation of one class by another.[1]

[1] There is a considerable literature on this subject, largely untranslated. As a beginning, the reader may be conveniently referred to Mr. Charles A. Beard's *Rise of American Civilization* and his work on the Constitution of the

ON DOING THE RIGHT THING

This at once cleared up all the anomalies
which I had found so troublesome. One could
see immediately, for instance, why the hunting
tribes and primitive peasants never formed a
State. Primitive peasants never made enough
of an economic accumulation to be worth stealing; they lived from hand to mouth. The
hunting tribes of North America never formed
a State, because the hunter was not exploitable.
There was no way to make another man hunt
for you; he would go off in the woods and
forget to come back; and if he were expropriated from certain hunting-grounds, he would
merely move on beyond them, the territory
being so large and the population so sparse.
Similarly, since the State's own primary intention was essentially criminal, one could see why
it cares only to monopolize crime, and not to
suppress it; this explained the anomalous behaviour of officials, and showed why it is that
in their public capacity, whatever their private
character, they appear necessarily as a profes-
sional-criminal class; and it further accounted

United States. After these he should study closely—for it is
hard reading—a small volume called *The State* by Professor
Franz Oppenheimer, of the University of Frankfort. It has
been well translated and is easily available.

for the fact that the State never moves disinterestedly for the general welfare, except grudgingly and under great pressure.

Again, one could perceive at once the basic misapprehension which forever nullifies the labors of Liberalism and Reform. It was once quite seriously suggested to me by some neighbours that I should go to Congress. I asked them why they wished me to do that, and they replied with some complimentary phrases about the satisfaction of having some one of a somewhat different type "amongst those damned rascals down there." "Yes, but," I said, "don't you see that it would be only a matter of a month or so—a very short time, anyway—before I should be a damned rascal, too?" No, they did not see this; they were rather taken aback; would I explain? "Suppose," I said, "that you put in a Sunday-school superintendent or a Y. M. C. A. secretary to run an assignation-house on Broadway. He might trim off some of the coarser fringes of the job, such as the badger game and the panel game, and put things in what Mayor Gaynor used to call a state of 'outward order and decency,' but he *must* run an assignation-house, or he would promptly hear from the owners." This was a new view to them, and they went away thoughtful.

Finally, one could perceive the reason for the matter that most puzzled me when I first observed a legislature in action, namely, the almost exclusive concern of legislative bodies with such measures as tend to take money out of one set of pockets and put it into another— the preoccupation with converting labour-made property into law-made property, and redistributing its ownership. The moment one becomes aware that just this, over and above a purely legal distribution of the ownership of natural resources, is what the State came into being for, and what it yet exists for, one immediately sees that the legislative bodies are acting altogether in character, and otherwise one cannot possibly give oneself an intelligent account of their behaviour.[1]

[1] When the Republican convention which nominated Mr. Harding was almost over, one of the party leaders met a man who was managing a kind of dark-horse, or one-horse, candidate, and said to him, "You can pack up that candidate of yours, and take him home now. I can't tell you who the next President will be; it will be one of three men, and I don't just yet know which. But I can tell you who the next Secretary of the Interior will be, and that is the important question, because there are still a few little

Speaking for a moment in the technical terms of economics, there are two general means whereby human beings can satisfy their needs and desires. One is by work—*i.e.*, by applying labour and capital to natural resources for the production of wealth, or to facilitating the exchange of labour-products. This is called the economic means. The other is by robbery—*i.e.*, the appropriation of the labour-products of others without compensation. This is called the political means. The State, considered functionally, may be described as *the organization of the political means,* enabling a comparatively small class of beneficiaries to satisfy their needs and desires through various delegations of the taxing power, which have no vestige of support in natural right, such as private land-ownership, tariffs, franchises, and the like.

It is a primary instinct of human nature to satisfy one's needs and desires with the least possible exertion; everyone tends by instinctive preference to use the political means rather than the economic means, if he can do so. The

___

things lying around loose that the boys want." I had this from a United States Senator, a Republican, who told it to me merely as a good story.

great desideratum in a tariff, for instance, is its license to rob the domestic consumer of the difference between the price of an article in a competitive and a non-competitive market. Every manufacturer would like this privilege of robbery if he could get it, and he takes steps to get it if he can, thus illustrating the powerful instinctive tendency to climb out of the exploited class, which lives by the economic means (exploited, because the cost of this privilege must finally come out of production, there being nowhere else for it to come from), and into the class which lives, wholly or partially, by the political means.

This instinct—and this alone—is what gives the State its almost impregnable strength. The moment one discerns this, one understands the almost universal disposition to glorify and magnify the State, and to insist upon the pretence that it is something which it is not—something, in fact, the direct opposite of what it is. One understands the complacent acceptance of one set of standards for the State's conduct, and another for private organizations; of one set for officials, and another for private persons. One understands at once the attitude of the

155

press, the Church and educational institutions, their careful inculcations of a specious patriotism, their nervous and vindictive proscriptions of opinion, doubt or even of question.   One sees why purely fictitious theories of the State and its activities are strongly, often fiercely and violently, insisted on; why the simple fundamentals of the very simple science of economics are shirked or veiled; and why, finally, those who really know what kind of thing they are promulgating, are loth to say so.

VIII

The outbreak of the war in 1914 found me entertaining the convictions that I have here outlined.   In the succeeding decade nothing has taken place to attenuate them, but quite the contrary.   Having set out only to tell the story of how I came by them, and not to expound them or indulge in any polemic for them, I may now bring this narrative to an end, with a word about their practical outcome.

It has sometimes been remarked as strange that I never joined in any agitation, or took the part of a propagandist for any movement against the State, especially at a time when I had an unexampled opportunity to do so. To do anything of the sort successfully, one must have more faith in such processes than I have, and one must also have a certain dogmatic turn of temperament, which I do not possess. To be quite candid, I was never much for evangelization; I am not sure enough that my opinions are right, and even if they were, a second-hand opinion is a poor possession. Reason and experience, I repeat, are all that determine our true beliefs. So I never greatly cared that people should think my way, or tried much to get them to do so. I should be glad if they *thought*—if their general turn, that is, were a little more for disinterested thinking, and a little less for impetuous action motivated by mere unconsidered prepossession; and what little I could ever do to promote disinterested thinking has, I believe, been done.

According to my observations (for which I claim nothing but that they are all I have to go by) inaction is better than wrong action or premature right action, and effective right action can only follow right thinking. "If a great change is to take place," said Edmund Burke, in his last words on the French Revolution, "the

minds of men *will be fitted to it.*" Otherwise
the thing does not turn out well; and the processes by which men's minds are fitted seem to
me untraceable and imponderable, the only certainty about them being that the share of any
one person, or any one movement, in determin-
ing them is extremely small. Various social
superstitions, such as magic, the divine right of
kings, the Calvinist teleology, and so on, have
stood out against many a vigorous frontal attack, and thrived on it; and when they finally
disappeared, it was not under attack. People
simply stopped thinking in those terms; no one
knew just when or why, and no one even was
much aware that they had stopped. So I think
it very possible that while we are saying, "Lo,
here!" and "Lo, there!" with our eye on this
or that revolution, usurpation, seizure of power,
or what not, the superstitions that surround the
State are quietly disappearing in the same way.[1]

My opinion of my own government and

[1] The most valuable result of the Russian Revolution is in
its liberation of the idea of the State as an engine of economic exploitation. In Denmark, according to a recent
article in *The English Review,* there is a considerable movement for a complete separation of politics from economics,
which, if effected, would of course mean the disappearance
of the State.

those who administer it can probably be inferred from what I have written. Mr. Jefferson said that if a centralization of power were ever effected at Washington, the United States would have the most corrupt government on earth. Comparisons are difficult, but I believe it has one that is thoroughly corrupt, flagitious, tyrannical, oppressive. Yet if it were in my power to pull down its whole structure overnight and set up another of my own devising—to abolish the State out of hand, and replace it by an organization of the economic means—I would not do it, for the minds of Americans are far from fitted to any such great change as this, and the effect would be only to lay open the way for the worse enormities of usurpation—possibly, who knows? with myself as the usurper! After the French Revolution, Napoleon!

Great and salutary social transformations, such as in the end do not cost more than they come to, are not effected by political shifts, by movements, by programs and platforms, least of all by violent revolutions, but by sound and disinterested thinking. The believers in action are numerous, their gospel is widely preached, they have many followers. Perhaps among

159

those who will see what I have here written, there are two or three who will agree with me that the believers in action do not need us— indeed, that if we joined them, we should be rather a dead weight for them to carry. We need not deny that their work is educative, or pinch pennies when we count up its cost in the inevitable reactions against it. We need only remark that our place and function in it are not apparent, and then proceed on our own way, first with the more obscure and extremely difficult work of clearing and illuminating our own minds, and second, with what occasional help we may offer to others whose faith, like our own, is set more on the regenerative power of thought than on the uncertain achievements of premature action.

On Doing the Right Thing

I

*F*OR my sins I had to spend a good deal of time in London lately, while an east wind was blowing; and under these depressing circumstances I had some notion of showing cause why the much-touted understanding between the English people and ours can never really exist. In spite of the Sulgrave Foundation, and of all the perfervid buncombe fired off at Pilgrims' dinners about cousinship, hands across the sea, common tradition, common ideals, and what Mr. Dooley called "th' common impulse f'r th' same money"—only that, I believe, is never mentioned—the two peoples will never understand each other as long as the world stands. There are many obscure, unregarded, and potent reasons against it; of which, for example, language is one. An American can make sounds to which an Englishman will attach approximately the same meaning that the American does, and hence each assumes that they have a common language, when actually they have nothing of the kind; that is to say, language does not enable a true

161

understanding of each other, but rather the contrary. Indeed, I believe that they would come nearer a real understanding if each had to learn a new language to get on with. There are many other reasons; and the reasons proceeding from recondite and apparently insignificant differences in training, habit, social and institutional procedure, and in the ordinary technique of living, account for more, I think, than those arising from weightier matters. As I said, I had the vagrant thought of tracing out and expounding some of these, but indolence interfered so persistently that it never was done and now, probably, never will be. One item on the list, however, recurs to me at the moment as worth salvaging for another purpose.

The English are addicted to a curious practice which is apprehended by an American only with great difficulty, and to which they give the rather conventional and indefinite name of "doing the Right Thing." The name at once brings to mind the late Sir Harry Johnston's fine novel; the best novel in that genre that has been written in our language since *The Way of All Flesh*. As far as I have been able to discover, the addiction to this practice pervades all classes of English society. The lower and middle classes do a good deal with it. The upper orders do not do as much with it as formerly, but they still do something; and even the official class does not quite escape. It is not a rationalised process, apparently, but on the contrary, one would perhaps say that it amounts to a kind of ritual. Given a certain set of circumstances, that is, an Englishman may be trusted to take a certain course of conduct, and to take it with energy, resolution and courage, for no reason in particular except to satisfy some inward sense of obligation. He may not, usually does not, have much light on the subject; doing the Right Thing may be far enough, indeed, from doing right. In other circumstances, too, where the inner sense is quiescent, he may do something much worse; but in *those* circumstances he is sure to carry through with a darkened and instinctive allegiance to what he believes to be the Right Thing.

II

Aside from the apparently irrational character of this addiction, what strikes the American as

odd is that casuistry has no place in it. When
an Englishman is bitten by a sense of the Right
Thing, it seems never to occur to him, for instance, to raise the question whether the Right
Thing, after it is done, will have enough practical importance to be worth doing. Again, it
seems never to occur to him to put a mere personal desire, however strong, in competition
with the Right Thing, and then to cast about
him for plausible ways of justifying himself in
following his desire. This uncommonly useful
faculty seems largely left out of the individual
Englishman, though collectively they show
more of it than any other nation—a curious
anomaly. The great French scholar, M. Nisard,
once complimented Matthew Arnold on belong-
ing to a nation that had the *savoir se gêner,* that
did not take a mere powerful desire to do something as a sufficient reason for doing it, but
could, if need be, bottle up the desire and cork
it down and go steadily on doing something
quite different. A dozen times a day one will
hear Englishmen mutter in an apologetic tone,
"Beastly bore, you know!—oh, dev'lish bore!—
but then, you know, one really must do the
Right Thing, mustn't one?" The formula and

the intonation never seem to vary, whether the matter at issue be utterly trivial or so important as to redetermine the whole course of a life.

I have always been interested in this trait of the English because of the connection which it immediately established in my mind with the principle of liberty. The theory of freedom rests on the doctrine of natural rights, and I have always held with the Declaration of Independence that this doctrine is a sound one, that mankind is endowed by its Creator with certain inalienable rights, and that one of them is liberty. But the world is fast going away from old-fashioned people of my kind, and I am told that this doctrine is debatable and now quite out of style; that nowadays almost no one believes that mankind has any natural rights at all, but that all the rights it enjoys are legal and conventional, and therefore properly subject to abridgement or suppression by the authority that confers them. Aside from theory and principle, however, this matter of freedom has a practical side which is undebatable, and about which, for some reason, very little is said; and this curious trait of the English serves admirably to bring it out.

165

A comparison drawn between the English and ourselves in the matter of devotion to the Right Thing seems at first sight unfavourable to Americans; and so, to some extent, it is. But the great point is that an Englishman keeps up his susceptibility to the Right Thing very largely because he is free to do so; because, that is, he is free to regulate so large a portion of his life in such way as he sees fit. In respect of control, the whole general area of human conduct may be laid off into three regions. First, there is the region in which conduct is controlled by law, *i.e.*, by force, by some form of outside compulsion. A man, for instance, may not murder or steal, because an organized power outside himself will withstand him before the fact, if possible, and make trouble for him after the fact. Second, there is the region of indifferent choice, where, for instance, a man may use one kind of soap or safety-razor rather than another. Third, there is the region where conduct is controlled by unenforced, self-imposed allegiance to moral or social considerations. In this region, for instance, one follows the rule of "women and children first," takes a long risk to get somebody out of a burning

166

house, or, like Sir Philip Sidney, refuses to slake one's own thirst when there is not water enough to go round.

Now, for whatever reason and however it came about, the Englishman's first region, the region of compulsion, is relatively small. He has not many laws to obey, and most of these relate to property; and what few of them bear on personal conduct are quite obviously bottomed on reason and good sense. He has too many laws, of course, and the present tendency over there, as everywhere, unhappily, is to multiply them; his situation is not ideal; but as compared with the American, he lives in an anarchist's paradise. Moreover, his second region, the region of indifferent choice, is relatively large because there is no great pressure of unintelligent and meddlesome public opinion to reduce it. Hence life in England is an affair of much more individual responsibility than here. With so little law and so much choice, the sense of things "up to" the individual is correspondingly quickened. Therefore the third region of conduct, the region controlled by allegiance to the Right Thing, is less trespassed upon and does not tend to shrink, but on the contrary, should normally tend to enlarge by the progressive transference of items from the first and second regions.

One is really astonished by the magnitude of the part that this sense of individual responsibility plays in the ordinary routine of living. Let me give two examples, one at each end of the scale of social importance. One Sunday morning in May, on the top deck of a Piccadilly bus, I saw a superb old specimen of sixty-five or so, looking precisely like du Maurier's cartoon of Sir Digby de Rigby. He wore a white plug hat with a two-inch black band, and a long shadbelly black coat, a purple-and-gold figured waistcoat, a high collar of antique design—something like a stock—a red tie, red socks, russet shoes and a pair of black-and-white checked pants such as no American has seen, I dare say, since the days of Christie's minstrels. Exclusive of jewelry, I estimated the whole layout at something like five hundred dollars; there was not a shoddy thread in it. He had a couple of ladies with him, and his conversation was entertaining and delightful; and as they disembarked opposite St. James's, I judged they were headed for church, the time being right

168

for it. The thing to be remarked is that no one commented on all this gorgeousness or paid any attention to it. If the old chap liked to dress that way, why, that was the way he liked to dress, and since he was not actually annoying anybody, it was up to him—why not? Anywhere in America, on the other hand, a man who got himself up like that to go to church would have attracted a charmed and enthusiastic rabble from the moment he put his nose out of doors.

So much for a small matter. At the other end of the scale of social importance, it is noteworthy that in England fornication is not a crime.[1] An unmarried couple may set up housekeeping in London and remain undisturbed by the law as long as they live, and if anyone else disturbs them the law will protect them; for English law protects those against whom it has no stated grievance, even though their conduct may not be exactly praiseworthy or popular. They may register at an hotel under their several names, and the law will not only leave them at peace but will protect their peace. Eng-

[1] I am told, to my astonishment, that neither is it a crime in the State of Maryland!

lish law interferes in sex relations only in the case of minors, to safeguard immaturity; and in the case of adultery, to safeguard a property-interest, or the vestiges of one. Other cases are put over into the third region of conduct and left subject to the individual sense of the Right Thing.

III

In America, on the other hand, the first region of conduct is egregiously expanded. I remember seeing recently a calculation that the poor American is staggering along under a burden of some two million laws; and obviously, where there are so many laws, it is hardly possible to conceive of any items of conduct escaping contact with one or more of them. Thus, the region where conduct is controlled by law so far encroaches upon the region of free choice and the region where conduct is controlled by a sense of the Right Thing, that there is precious little left of either. What is left, moreover, is still further attenuated by the pressure of a public opinion whose energy and zeal are in direct ratio to its meddlesomeness and ignorance. The complaint of critics against what they call our "standardisation" is a complaint against this pressure; and it is so just, and its ground so obvious, that it needs no reiteration here. The only thing I wish to remark is the serious and debilitating deterioration of individual responsibility under this state of affairs. In this respect, living in America is like serving in the army; ninety per cent of conduct is prescribed by law and the remaining ten per cent by the *esprit du corps,* with the consequence that opportunity for free choice in conduct is practically abolished. This falls in very well with the indolent disposition of human nature to regard responsibility as onerous and to dodge it when possible; but it is debilitating, and a civilisation organised upon this absence of responsibility is pulpy and unsound.

Indeed, a vague sense of this unsoundness has lately been pervading our people; but it has expressed itself, so far, only in a panicky hospitality to political nostrums of the "liberal and progressive" type, whose tendency is all to aggravate the complaint that they are advertised to remedy. To get a correct measure of our Liberals and Progressives, all one need do is to observe that they contemplate a further enlarge-

ment of the first region of conduct; they would
have us even more closely controlled by law
than we already are! They are more for this,
more for indulging an ignorant and licentious
zeal for law-mongering than even the hide-
bound Tories. As well as I can make out,
Chief Justice Taft or Mr. Coolidge or even Mr.
Hughes would organize far less trespass on the
second and third regions of conduct, if they
had their way, than would the late Mr. Roosevelt or the late Senator La Follette; and certainly, of all men I ever knew, the Liberals
of my acquaintance have the greatest nervous
horror of freedom, the most inveterate and
pusillanimous dread of contemplating the ideal
picture of mankind existing in free and volun-
tary association. From such as these, then,
nothing may be expected but an exacerbation of
the social trouble whereof they seem able to
contemplate nothing but the symptoms.

IV

It is not to the point to protest, for example,
that Mr. Roosevelt's laws or Senator La Follette's would all be good laws, that their en-
largements of the first region of conduct would

all be for our own good. The point is that *any* enlargement, good or bad, reduces the scope of individual responsibility, and thus retards and cripples the education which can be a product of nothing but the free exercise of moral judgment. Like the discipline of the army, again, any such enlargement, good or bad, depraves this education into a mere routine of mechanical assent. The profound instinct against being "done for our own good" even by an Aristides—the instinct so miserably misinterpreted by our Liberals and Progressives—is wholly sound. Men are aware of the need of this moral experience as a condition of growth, and they are aware, too, that anything tending to ease it off from them, even for their own good, is to be profoundly distrusted.

The practical reason for freedom, then, is that freedom seems to be the only condition under which any kind of substantial moral fibre can be developed. Everything else has been tried, world without end. Going dead against reason and experience, we have tried law, compulsion and authoritarianism of various kinds, and the result is nothing to be proud of. Americans have many virtues of their own, which

173

I would be the last to belittle or disparage, but the power of quick and independent moral judgment is not one of them. In suggesting that we try freedom, therefore, the anarchist and individualist has a strictly practical aim. He aims at the production of a race of responsible beings. He wants more room for the *savoir se gêner*, more scope for the *noblesse oblige*, a larger place for the sense of the Right Thing. If our legalists and authoritarians could once get this well through their heads, they would save themselves a vast deal of silly insistence on a half-truth and upon the *suppressio veri*, which is the meanest and lowest form of misrepresentation. Freedom, for example, as they keep insisting, undoubtedly means freedom to drink oneself to death. The anarchist grants this at once; but at the same time he points out that it also means freedom to say with the gravedigger in "Les Misérables," "I have studied, I have graduated; I never drink." It unquestionably means freedom to go on without any code of morals at all; but it also means freedom to rationalise, construct and adhere to a code of one's own. The anarchist presses the point invariably overlooked,

174

that freedom to do the one without correla-
tive freedom to do the other is impossible; and
that just here comes in the moral education
which legalism and authoritarianism, with their
denial of freedom, can never furnish.

The anarchist is not interested in any nar-
rower or more personal view of human conduct.   Believing, for example, that man should
be wholly free to be sober or to be a sot, his
eye is not caught and exclusively engaged by
the spectacle of sots, but instead he points to
those who are responsibly sober, sober by a self-
imposed standard of conduct, and asserts his
conviction that the future belongs to them
rather than to the sots.   He believes in absolute
freedom in sex-relations; yet when the eman-
cipated man or woman goes simply on the loose,
to wallow along at the mercy of raw sensation
from one squalid little *Schweinerei* to another,
he is not interested in their panegyrics upon
freedom.   Instead, he is bored and annoyed,
and sometimes casts hankering glances towards
the trusty fowling-piece, vainly wishing he
could convince himself that a low rake or a dirty
drab is worth the price of a dozen buckshot.
Then he turns to contemplate those men and

women who are responsibly decent, decent by a strong, fine, self-sprung consciousness of the Right Thing, and he declares his conviction that the future lies with them.

The anarchist, moreover, does not believe that any considerable proportion of human beings will promptly turn into rogues and adventuresses, sots and strumpets, as soon as they find themselves free to do so; but quite the contrary. It seems to be a fond notion with the legalists and authoritarians that the vast majority of mankind would at once begin to thieve and murder and generally misconduct itself if the restraints of law and authority were removed. The anarchist, whose opportunities to view mankind in its natural state are perhaps as good as the legalist's, regards this belief as devoid of foundation. Seeing how much evildoing is directly chargeable to economic pressure alone, the anarchist maintains that the legalists and authoritarians have no proper means of estimating natural human goodness until they postulate it as functioning in a state of economic freedom. They have no proper estimate of the common run of moral sensitiveness, strictness and scrupulousness until they postu-

late the moral sense as functioning in a state
of social and political freedom based upon economic freedom.   Indeed, considering the disabilities put upon this sense, and the incessant
organised efforts to deform and weaken it, the
anarchist makes bold to marvel that it functions
as well as it does.

v

But I have no intention of digressing into
a syllabus of anarchist philosophy.   I have
thought it worth while to write out the forego-
ing thoughts, however, merely to make clear
that there is a practical side to this philosophy,
as well as a theoretical side, and one which is
not perhaps wholly unworthy of consideration.
The anarchist does not want economic freedom
for the sake of shifting a dollar or two from
one man's pocket to another's; or social freedom
for the sake of rollicking in detestable license;
or political freedom for the sake of a mere rash
and restless experimentation in system-making.
His desire for freedom has but the one practical object, *i.e.,* that men may become as good
and decent, as elevated and noble, as they
might be and really wish to be.   Reason, experi-

177

ence and observation lead him to the conviction that under absolute and unqualified freedom they can, and rather promptly will, educate themselves to this desirable end; but that so long as they are to the least degree dominated by legalism and authoritarianism, they never can.

A Study in Manners

I

AMERICAN history has been of late so largely rediscovered and rewritten that one would hardly imagine there were many left to share the late Mr. Harding's amiable illusions about the Founding Fathers. Yet there must be some, for in the campaign of 1924 I was present when one of the candidates got a rousing hand of applause for telling his audience that the Fathers had established a government of the people, for the people, and by the people! I was greatly tempted to ask him whether he had ever heard of a publication called the *Federalist,* and if not, whether he would like to borrow my old calf-bound copy and browse around in it a little here and there, before committing himself further to this preposterous proposition.

The Founding Fathers, in fact, did no such thing—far from it. They had the greatest horror of popular government; they dreaded it like the plague. A view of the Constitutional Convention of 1787 as a disinterested and high-

179

minded rivalry between two abstract political theories is very pretty, but sheer fiction. The Fathers were not theorists. There was no discount on their ability; in that respect they were one of the most extraordinary and remarkable groups that the world ever saw; but their disinterestedness was not, perhaps, quite what the romantic tradition of the school-books cracks it up to be. As Mr. Dooley remarked, they "were mostly in the fish-ile business," and the Constitutional Convention was made up of hardheaded and wary brethren who were not strong on abstractions but were very clear about what they wanted and uncommonly skilful in framing the right kind of air-tight charter for getting it. Their enthusiasm for popular government was about as strong as the late Judge Gary's or Mr. Pierpont Morgan's, and had the same motive. As a matter of fact, government is at this moment much nearer the hands of the people than the Founding Fathers left it, or than they ever intended it should be.

A coarse and indiscriminate glorification of the Fathers does great disservice to their memory because, among other reasons, it tends to obscure the really good and fine things which they occasionally did. The school-book's picture of them is like a Gothic fresco; everything is flat, without any perspective or relief. If all the Fathers were uniformly noble, public-spirited, and disinterested all the time, then all their acts were equipollent and none more impressive than another. When the average of nobility and disinterestedness is one hundred per cent twenty-four hours a day, even a Founding Father cannot go over it. If, however, revaluation brings the average down somewhere near erring humanity's normal figure, the occasional hundred per cent achievement stands out in proper perspective and can be appraised accordingly. In the course of a casual occupation with the doings of the Fathers, I lately happened on one of these achievements which moved me profoundly; and yet the act itself did not, I think, stir my imagination as much as did the reason that the Father gave for doing it.

In the year 1800, the year of the great final contest between the Federalists and the Republicans, the outgoing legislature of New York was Federalist and the newly-elected legislature was anti-Federalist. Since the stripe of the presidential electors was at that time determined by that of the legislature, this boded great danger to the Federalist national ticket; it threatened to seat Mr. Jefferson in the presidential chair; and this prospect so frightened Alexander Hamilton that he addressed a letter to the Governor of New York, who was then John Jay, urging him to recall the adjourned legislature, for the purpose of enacting a clever measure to defeat the will of the people and save the national election for the party.

This letter was a model of strength and speciousness. Hamilton assured Governor Jay that "in times like these in which we live, it will not do to be over-scrupulous," and that "the scruples of delicacy and propriety, as relative to a common course of things, ought to yield to the extraordinary nature of the crisis. They ought not to hinder the taking of a legal and constitutional step to prevent an atheist in religion and a fanatic in politics from getting possession of the helm of state." Hamilton knew his man, and he laid all the stress he could upon the one point that he knew would most of all stick in the Governor's craw; but to no purpose. Governor Jay did not move in the matter. There is no record, as far as I know, that he even acknowledged Hamilton's letter. After his death, nearly thirty years later, it was found among his papers, inscribed, "Proposing a measure for party purposes, which I do not think it would be becoming to adopt."

Governor Jay had unusual ability and the most nearly flawless character, probably, of any man in the public life of that time. Mr. Beveridge, in his biography of Marshall, characterises him sympathetically as "the learned and gentle Jay." In principle he was as strong a Federalist as Hamilton himself, for by all the force of birth, education, and circumstances he was an aristocrat. Quite conscientiously, he was one of those whom Mr. Jefferson described under a striking figure, as believing that some of mankind were born with saddles on their backs, and others born booted and spurred to ride them. While not a purblind Anglophile, he had as long as possible favored a mild and conciliatory policy toward England in the pre-Revolutionary period, and in 1794 he had been burned in effigy all over the country for the execution of the treaty which bears his name. He had a deep distrust of popular government, and viewed the prospective triumph of Mr. Jefferson, the "fanatic in politics," with apprehension and distaste. After Mr. Jefferson's election, indeed, he refused further preferment, turned his back upon public life, and though at the height of his powers, passed the rest of his days in retirement.

Why may not a wayward scion of his stock say of him what any radical-minded outsider would surely say, that he was a benighted old Tory? He could quite legally and constitutionally have made the move that Hamilton implored him to make, for the old legislature still had tenure of office for seven or eight weeks. If he had done so, no doubt, public sentiment in New York State would have run pretty high; but that need not have concerned him, for, with his own party continued in power at Washington, the Administration would have taken royal good care of him and given him his pick of patronage. Every predilection of his own was in favour of Hamilton's suggestion. A devout man, he might well have let the end justify the means of keeping a person of Mr. Jefferson's well-known unorthodoxy out of the Presidency. Yet he looked at the opportunity and passed it by in silence because

184

he did not think it would be becoming to embrace it.

II

One rubs one's eyes in astonishment. What an extraordinary reason to assign for a decision of such profound political significance! What an extraordinary standard by which to appraise political conduct! That an act is illegal might conceivably give some shadow of reason why a politician should object to it. The exceptional politician might even, indeed, in an atrabilious moment, object to an act because he found it immoral or dishonest. Objection, however, to an act which is neither illegal nor dishonest, merely because it is *unbecoming*—this represents a distinction which, to put it gently, few politicians of today could be expected to draw under any circumstances, let alone such circumstances as pressed so powerfully upon Governor Jay.

Let us suppose a case that would stand in some kind of rough correspondence. Governor Smith is said to be one of the most honest and disinterested men in our public life, and Senator La Follette occupied, in the campaign of 1924, a position which in one or two essential respects

185

resembled that of Mr. Jefferson's in 1800. Suppose now that Senator La Follette's election, as far as one could see, had hung on the question whether Governor Smith would or would not turn a political trick that was legal and regular enough, but *unbecoming*—well, without the least wish to disparage Governor Smith, whom I do not know and never saw, and whose public acts as a rule impress me favourably, I merely ask what, in such a case, might one expect? In the campaign of 1924, Senator La Follette was almost as much dreaded, execrated and maligned as was Mr. Jefferson in the campaign of 1800. Would Governor Smith consent to see his own party lose a national election, and the Cagliostro of politics take the Presidency, rather than do something that had no more against it than mere shabbiness and indecency?

One might make use of Governor Jay's fine action, I suppose, to show how disreputably low the personnel of our public service has fallen in these degenerate days, and how hard we should all work to get good men in office and to keep them there. Yet for one reason or another, I have somewhat of the Psalmist's diffidence about meddling with these "great matters which are too high for me," preferring to turn all that kind of thing over to the Liberal publicists. *Beati pauperes spiritu!*—I bring this incident forward only because I myself greatly enjoy dwelling on it; and I enjoy dwelling on it because it intimates so clearly the enormous power that resides in a proper sense of what is *becoming*, and the intense satisfaction that one gets out of cultivating and indulging this sense. The incident, in short, provides an excellent study in manners, with which the austere Liberal publicist, absorbed in his great task of educating other people, would probably be impatient, and disdain it as mere shillyshallying, but which is nevertheless not without profit to those humbler spirits, like myself, who are still trying to educate themselves.

The word *manners*, unfortunately, has come to be understood as a synonym for deportment; it includes deportment, of course, but it reaches much further. Properly speaking, it covers the entire range of conduct outside the regions where law and morals have control. Goethe, with extraordinary penetration, called attention to certain "conquests which culture has made over nature," and to the importance of observ-

187

ing and maintaining them. Law and morals take cognizance, though very imperfectly and often improperly, of some of these culture-conquests; the rest are in the purview of manners.

In speaking of these culture-conquests as having been won from nature, Goethe's choice of terms is striking and serviceable, but not exact. One would prefer to say, perhaps, that they are conquests which culture has made over the primitive, rather than over nature; for what culture has actually done is to modify certain primitive rights, or cause them to be superseded, through the gradual disclosure of other rights which may be regarded as even more nearly natural, since they comport better with the disposition developed in man as he becomes progressively humanized in society. Culture so exhibits the appropriateness of loyalty to these rights as to inculcate upon us a devotion to them and lead us to acknowledge their validity.

The primitive doctrine of property, for example, now survives in an unmodified form hardly anywhere outside the jungle and the Foreign Offices of imperialist nations. St. Paul, portraying under his admirable figure of the "two selves," the bitter contest that goes on in the individual between the lower and apparent self, governed by what he so finely calls "the suggestions of the flesh and of the *current thoughts*,"[1] the extemporized, capricious and unconsidered promptings of primitive desire, and the higher and real self, governed by loyalties to which all such impulses are wholly repugnant—here St. Paul, I say, is far more accurate and explicit in his account of the operations of culture than Goethe. Yet the great critic's meaning is clear enough. In stealing an inventor's purse, let us say, one must reckon with the law; in stealing his idea, one must reckon with the sense of morals, with the common conscience of mankind; in buying up and suppressing his idea or in exploiting it without adequate compensation, one must reckon with the sense of manners, with the fine and high perceptions established by culture, to which such transactions at once appear mean and low. When Baron Tauchnitz paid full royalties to foreign authors whose works he republished before the days of international copyright, he was governed by a sense of manners; for no

[1] θελήματα τῆς σαρκὸς καὶ τῶν διανοίων—Eph. II: 3.

189

law compelled him to pay anything, and the morals of trade would have been quite satisfied if he had paid whatever he chose to pay.

Governor Jay's attitude towards Hamilton's suggestion may be called not only a study in manners, but, with certain explanations carefully made and certain discriminations fully understood, it may justly be called a study in Tory manners. This does not by any manner of means intimate that all Tories have a keen sense of manners, or that the Tory spirit has any natural monopoly of manners, to the exclusion of the radical and liberal spirit. On the contrary, English history exhibits one of the very finest examples of manners in the person of one who was an aristocrat, indeed, but withal, for his time, a great radical—a kind of British Jefferson. By some master-stroke of unconscious irony, the statue of Falkland stands today in a drooping attitude, an attitude of almost despairing despondency—and no wonder! —at the inner entrance to the Houses of Parliament! Lucius Cary, Viscount Falkland, was Secretary of State for a year during the difficult and troubled period just preceding the Civil War. Those who do not know his melancholy

and fascinating history do not know the best
that England can do in the way of dignifying
and ennobling herself in the men she produces.
Throughout his tenure of office, Falkland refused either to employ spies or to open letters!
Horace Walpole speaks of this as "evincing
debility of mind," quite as plausibly as Hamilton admonished Governor Jay that "in times
like these in which we live, it will not do to be
over-scrupulous."

But though manners be not a Tory peculium,
it is indisputable that a high sense of manners,
a fine and delicate perception in matters of
conduct, and the supporting strength of character that gives practical effect to both, have
been most highly developed and most powerfully propagated by an aristocracy; and an aristocracy is always almost solidly Tory.   Where
one finds, as in Falkland, or Mr. Jefferson, radical principles and ideals combined with Tory
manners, there, of course, one sees about the
best that human nature is capable of producing;
but such characters are all too seldom met with.
I hasten to add that there is no natural reason
why the qualities that I have mentioned should
not be developed as highly in a democracy, if

and when democracy ever comes to pass,[1] and I believe they will be much more highly developed; but the fact is that they have been chiefly developed in our modern civilisation through an aristocracy. Indeed, since about all the good one can say of an aristocracy is that it has done this, and since aristocracy is at a pretty heavy discount just now, we can probably afford generosity enough to remember with gratitude that it was no trifling service.

It is interesting to remark that a sense of manners, delicacy of perception in matters of conduct, and the strength of character which regularly and resolutely enforces upon oneself their findings, seem to attain their best development in the absence or abeyance of law. Our

[1] I wish to complain against the common and culpable misuse of the term democracy as a synonym for republicanism. Time and again one hears persons who should know better, talk about democracy in this country, for example, as if something like it really existed here. They discuss "democracy on trial," "democracy's weakness," and so on, when it is perfectly clear that they refer only to the political system known properly as republicanism. The fact is that republicanism, which is a system theoretically based on the right of individual self-expression in politics, has as yet done but little for democracy, and that democracy is less developed in some republican countries, as France and the United States, than in some others, like Denmark, whose political system is nominally non-republican.

192

Indian hunting tribes, for example, never formed a State, and lived without law or government; and there is no end of testimony to the extraordinary and impressive development of manners and the sense of manners, that prevailed among them. Among those peoples which for one reason or another we choose to call civilised, we see a somewhat similar development in a hereditary governing class which can manage the law pretty much to suit itself and hence exists largely above the law. The aristocratic system was in general an incompetent one and its breakdown was inevitable; yet there is some good in the worst of systems, and the good of the aristocratic system was in the stimulation it gave to the sense of manners as a kind of law in itself, outside the purview of either statutory law or morals. It is chiefly to the extra-legal tradition which his hereditary governing class worked out for itself and followed with some degree of faithfulness, that the ordinary Englishman today owes his instinctive power of appraisal, such as it is, in the category of things which he vaguely yet stoutly assures you "aren't done," or which he briefly characterises as "dam' low." Under republicanism this advantage disappears, and the sense of manners, no longer cultivable by this indirect and somewhat adventitious means, must, if cultivated at all, be cultivated more directly and purposefully. Now, there is no doubt, I think, that the sum total of our educational processes does not tend that way. One may be subjected to the resultant influence of our schools, newspapers, pulpits, colleges, average family life, average social life, without gaining any very clear conception of the sense of manners as a kind of law in itself, and indeed without having one's intellectual curiosity much stirred by any consideration of manners, one way or the other.

Half a century ago Ernest Renan acutely pointed out that countries like the United States, which tolerate such imperfections in their educational processes, "would long have to expiate their fault by their intellectual mediocrity, *the vulgarity of their manners,* their superficial spirit, their failure in general intelligence." It would seem that his forecast was substantially accurate; there is testimony to it not only in a rather widespread general restlessness and dissatisfaction with the quality of life lived in the

United States, but also in innumerable specific complaints that drive us to adopt various forms of censorship and legal regulation. It is also worthy of remark, perhaps, that in our common speech we have constructed a considerable glossary of terms like "getting by," "putting it across," and "putting something over," which intimate the extremely narrow jurisdiction that we habitually assign to manners, and the correspondingly attenuated authority that we attach to the sense of manners.

It may be a form of good one hundred per cent Americanism, I suppose, to declare stoutly that in so enlightened and progressive a civilisation as ours, any abstract consideration of manners is impracticable and superfluous, and that we should deal pragmatically with our standard of manners by progressive improvisation as we go along. While visiting an exhibition of paintings with a friend the other day, I raised some questions of taste and style, and my friend said with a strong air of finality, "But what is taste? Simply your taste, my taste, anybody's taste." In the view of this naïve cynicism, obviously, a general duty to taste is fully discharged when each crude per-

son cleaves happily to what he likes, without
troubling himself to ask whether he ought to
like it; in other words, without admitting the
operation of an artistic conscience, or bethinking
himself that the best reason and spirit of the
race may have something to say in the premises, and that what it says may conceivably be
worth attention. Similarly, too, it may be
thought that a general duty to manners is fully
discharged when each crude person follows the
motions of the herd, or so much of them as his
lower and apparent self may elect to follow,
and regards his obligations as no more rational
or binding, at best, than those of mere fashion.

Yet a cautious old pedant like myself finds
it hard to swallow this, because general human
experience seems to be against it. Try as he
may, he cannot get quite away from the notion
that matters like these are not finally to be settled in this happy-go-lucky way, by the whim
of each raw person's ordinary self, but by what
Aristotle calls "the determination of the judicious"—the judicious being those who have
disciplined themselves to take the largest view
of general human experience and who have
become most sensitive to its testimony. There

196

is a fundamental self-preserving instinct in
humanity, which in the end comes out for what
is truly lovely, truly elevated and becoming, and
will not be permanently satisfied without it.
Even that strange son of Balaam, the *homme
sensuel moyen,* from Horace down to Mr. Otto
H. Kahn, gives this instinct his blessing if not
his obedience.   It is precisely this instinct which
our sturdy Americanism, with its blind insistence
on the sanction of law and morals for the exclusive control of conduct, and its equally blind
disregard of manners, and of the sense of manners as a law in itself, fails to take into account;
and the consequence is that our republican civilisation has an obvious and disconcerting ele-
ment of instability which it need not and should
not have.   With aristocracy gone, and republicanism thrown wholly on its own resources in
matters of this kind, one would say that it
behooves a republic to become aware of the edi-
fying and salutary power resident in a well-developed sense of manners, and to take steps
towards concentrating this power and making it
effective; and the very first of these steps,
logically, is for all of us who have somewhat to
do with general education—teachers, editors,

197

preachers, critics, essayists, dramatists, novelists, lecturers—firmly to dissociate from law and morals all courses of conduct that do not belong there, and as firmly to associate them in the category of manners.

III

This, I say, is logical; for what is the use of forever trying mechanically to apply sanctions which are by nature inapplicable and which anyone can see are simply grotesque in their inapplicability, while neglecting others which can be applied intelligently and appropriately? To make a thing illegal, or to put it down as immoral, by sheer fiat, in the face of an instinct which declares it properly to be neither, does not get one very far in the discouragement of its practice. Cardinal Hayes and Dr. John Roach Straton, for instance, have lately been complaining about the "morals of the young," as exhibited in their amusements, habits of conversation, irregular sex relations, the literature they choose to read and the plays they choose to see. Instinct testifies that in all this these gentlemen have no ground of complaint whatever against morals, and are talking blank nonsense; but that they have an impregnable ground of complaint against manners. If therefore they shifted their ground, they might hope to make an impression which they will never make from where they stand, for they would then have the natural truth of things working with them instead of against them.

When Mr. Taft came out of the White House, he refused to practice his profession and, though a poor man, turned his back upon the emoluments that would have come to him through his prestige as an ex-President. His successor, Mr. Wilson, did the opposite. It is absurd to say that Mr. Taft here showed himself more moral than Mr. Wilson, for morals have no jurisdiction in the premises. Again, when Mr. Jefferson became President, he made it a rule never to take a present from anyone under any circumstances. Other Presidents have not felt it incumbent upon them to do this; but it is utter nonsense to disparage them, or to praise Mr. Jefferson, on the score of morality. Mr. Taft and Mr. Jefferson simply gave an example of admirable manners, of a high and fine perception in matters of conduct, combined with the strength of character to enforce its findings upon themselves at whatever sacrifice; and the others did not.

A symposium dealing with the subject of sexual insurrection has been lately published under the title, "Our Changing Morality." Its original serial title, I believe, was "New Morals for Old." It rather reminded me of Bishop Pontoppidan's chapter on owls in Iceland, for from end to end of the symposium I could find nothing that had any natural connexion with morals, new or old, changing or fixed. Instinct testifies that there is absolutely nothing in the relations of either man or woman with any paramour or syndicate of paramours, which comes properly under the contemplation of morals; and hence any attempt to place them there is nugatory. These matters come properly under the scrutiny, much more effective because wholly appropriate, much more searching because wholly self-imposed, of high-mindedness, delicacy of feeling and perception—in a word, of manners.

Once we give up the pestilent assumption that the only effective sanctions of conduct are those of law and morals, and begin to delimit clearly the field of manners, we shall be by way of discovering how powerful and how easily communicable the sense of manners is, and how efficiently it operates in the very regions where law and morals have so notoriously proven themselves inert. The authority of law and morals does relatively little to build up personal dignity, responsibility and self-respect, while the authority of manners does much. The sacrifices and renunciations exacted by the one authority differ in quality from those exacted by the other, and one assents to them in a different spirit. In a habitual and sensitive regard to the demands of manners, one "lives from a greater depth of being." All this is matter of experience; anyone can try it for himself and find out that it is so. The trouble is that an enormously exaggerated stress on law and morals gives little encouragement to make the trial. It is easier, in a society like ours, to do as the rest do, and mechanically refer all conduct to the sanction of law and morals without troubling oneself to question its applicability or to cast about for a more appropriate authority.

This, in fact, is what our society appears to be doing. It seems competent, therefore, for even the humblest republican intellect to sug-

gest that we may be incurring pretty serious
damage through sheer unintelligent indisposi-
tion to call things by their right names and take
hold of them by the right handles; and that if
we stopped our heavy overdoing of law and
morals long enough to give consideration to
manners, and to the sense of manners as an
arbiter of conduct, we might considerably better
our prospects.   Mr. Jefferson—if I may once
more cite that poor old devotee of so many
decrepit superstitions—Mr. Jefferson remarked
that "it is the *manners* and spirit of a people
which preserve a republic in vigor.   A degen-
eracy in these is a canker which soon eats to the
heart of its laws and constitution."   I also venture to emphasise for special notice by the
Americanisers and hundred-per-centers among
us, the observation of Edmund Burke that
"there ought to be a system of *manners* in every
nation which a well-formed mind would be disposed to relish.   For us to love our country, our
country ought to be lovely."

Thoughts on Revolution

ONE afternoon last December as I was passing by a café in Paris I got a jovial hail from an old friend whom I had not seen for years. He was about the last person in the world that I should have expected to turn up in Paris, for I thought he was in Russia, where, indeed, he had been for two years, and was but just out; he had come straight from Petersburg to Paris the week before. I was a bit pressed for time at the moment, so we agreed to meet at noon on the day following; and he left me with the remark, which struck me as a little odd, though I did not pay much attention to it at the time, that if anything interfered I could always find him at that café, "rain or shine, sick or well, drunk or sober."

Next day, in the course of conversation about Russian affairs, he said, "What I told you yesterday was literally true. I haven't stirred out of that café, except to sleep, since I came to Paris. I don't want to go to the theatre, see sights, or hear music. Plenty of all that in

203

Russia.   But to be surrounded by people who
are just talking, talking at leisure, talking about
all sorts of matters of common social interest
—that's what I haven't had for two years.

"I'll tell you how it is," he went on.   "There
is plenty of good in modern Russia, and a great
deal to be said for the Government.   Any student of history can see that.   They have the
same old stupid, exasperating bureaucracy that
they have always had, but at that, it isn't any
worse than bureaucracy anywhere else, at home,
or here in France, or ——"

"Are they disinterested?" I broke in.

"Absolutely, I believe," he said.   "I am sure
of it.   They do a lot of stupid things.   Their
terrorist policy, for instance, is silly and unneces-
sary—they are safe enough.   But again, like us
Americans, or like the French, or any other of
the old-line governments, it's the only method
they seem to understand.   I can't put on any
airs about them, the Lord knows, when I think
of Palmer and Burleson, Funston and Hell-
roaring Jake Smith, and all the rest of our thin
·red line of heroes.   I only wish they wouldn't
do it, for, as I say, they don't need to.   They

have been smart enough to drop most of the
old-line fool methods, and found there was no
end of popular prestige in it, so I should think
they would drop them all. In diplomacy, for
instance, I suppose you noticed how Litvinov
stood the League of Nations on its head at
Geneva the other day, by calling its bluff about
disarmament. The press and politicians of the
other countries could only blackguard him—
they knew he was showing them up, and all they
could do about it was to lose their temper. But
I have lived close to the Russian Government
for two years, and while they do a good deal
that I don't like, I am sure there isn't a man
in it who is not bent solely on doing his level
best for the masses of Russia."

My friend paused a moment to discourage
a fat crop-eared cat that was sharpening its
claws on his trouser-leg. Then he proceeded:

"However, it isn't particularly Russia that I
am thinking about, but revolutions in general.
I am all for them, you understand. We ought
to have a lot more of them than we do. Thomas
Jefferson struck twelve as usual when he said,
God forbid that America should ever go twenty
years without some such blow-up as Shays's

Rebellion. He could see the future as well as we can see the past. Who couldn't see it? An enormous territory, rich as soap-grease, a scrawny thin population bent on looting it to the limit, a small fraction of the population blessed with the low sagacity to manage the Government into letting them get all four feet in the trough to crowd out the others—and there you are! I tell you, Thomas had his head properly screwed on when he said that once in twenty years would be about right, though if I had been in his place, I'd have taken a chance and made it ten."

"Have a drink, Jim," I suggested. "Don't be so blue. Remember the American Legion met here the other day—this is hallowed ground! Take a hooker of this French beer, and cheer up!"

We compromised on some French coffee, and my companion took up his parable again:

"I am not so bloodthirsty as you think. I'll explain all that presently. But getting back where we started, I don't doubt that society has made some progress in the technique of revolution. There isn't nearly so much bloodshed, for one thing. Compare the Russian Revolution

with the French, or with any of its major predecessors in history, and you may almost say it
was bloodless. Again, I think that in any future
revolution the works of art will be safe, the
temples of art and science, the interesting vestiges of antiquity. The Russian Revolution
carefully spared all those, carefully kept them
out of harm's way. We shan't have any more
vandalism like that of Cromwell's soldiers, or
like what took place in Northern Flanders, or
during the French Revolution itself. When
you think of what those fellows did to the whole
tangible apparatus of beauty, and to the romance and poetry of life, you have to cut the
cards with yourself to decide whether the
French Revolution was worth the price. But
from now on, as I say, I believe all those things
will be safe.

"But will the *cafés* be safe?" My friend
suddenly shook the forefinger of emphasis under my nose, and then gave his arm a wide
sweep to include all the little groups of chat-
ting fellow-loungers about us. "Will all *this*
be safe? This leisurely free conversation on
any topic that the human mind is heir to, the
quiet infiltration of ideas and notions, not very

important, maybe, but not so unimportant either
when you understand how humanizing the
process is and how much it has to do with building up the social sense. Look at all these people
here, all talking, and probably no two groups
talking about the same thing. I dare say none
of it is of the kind that moves mountains exactly, and yet would you say that all this talk
makes for inefficiency? Well, yes and no. It
does for robots, but not for human beings. It
may not help build up the Industrial State, or
round off a Country Fit for Heroes to Live in,
but it goes a long way to make life a lovely
reality.

"Well, will *that* be safe? It wasn't safe in
Russia. All that kind of thing is dead and gone
—hopelessly busted, like the old Flemish
stained glass. There you get the real savagery
of a revolution! When you have a revolution
on, or when you are consolidating the gains of
a revolution—worse then, because it takes
longer—you have an utter wreckage of the human spirit and of the humane life, even if not
a drop of blood has been shed, or a dollar's
worth of property destroyed.

"It is the old story in Russia. Nobody can

think or talk about anything but the Revolution. Science, literature, music, drama, painting, poetry, religion, social life, all follow the flag. You bet they do, just as they did in France in 1789. In other words, every blessed value in human life is adulterated. Speak to anyone about the permanent unchanging values in any activity of the human spirit, and he will come right back at you with his infernal little set of arbitrary values, as prompt and smug as a Kansas prohibitionist. Where two or three are gathered together you'd think you were at a committee meeting of the Anti-Saloon League. There is wonderful art in Petersburg—Moscow, too—by George! you ought to see what they've got! But they don't put their mind on it, you know. They merely salvaged it. Talk about it, and they sidetrack you right away on the Art of the Revolution. So you get the Music of the Revolution, the Literature of the Revolution, and so on—every avenue of excursion for the human spirit is cluttered up with flubdubbery about the dam' old Revolution. It gives one a bright idea of what life must have been like amidst all the rabid nonsense that was uttered in Philadelphia in 1789 by noisy numskulls who called each other 'citizen,' and wore cockades. Revolution simply defiles the spiritual atmosphere of a country, and no social life worthy of the name—nothing that is any life at all—can flourish."

"In other words," I said, "any kind of social life that commands a civilized person's respect is possible only in a fairly stable order of things."

"Just so," he said. "It's no discovery; it has been observed before. But the fact has slipped down so far out of sight that if it isn't dragged up and posted as a warning pretty soon, civilization-building will become a lost art."

"But that's just where our country comes in to make the world safe for civilization, don't you see?" I replied. "There's a stable order of things for you!—rich, powerful, influential, unshakable! We have a benevolent, far-seeing plutocracy and a prosperous, contented proletariat. Can you imagine greater stability than that? Didn't Mr. Hoover report to the President the other day that real wages were never so high at any time or any place in the world? I assure you that the very last bulwark—if it comes to that—against world-wide revolution will be found in the Mississippi Valley. So we are free from all those preoccupations, and we can help restore the art of civilization-building in those less happy regions where its exercise is temporarily suspended. I make no doubt that this is our destiny, our great mission."

My companion had been sitting with his chair a-tilt. While I was speaking, he slowly brought it down on all-fours and looked at me steadily in the face with an expression of the blankest amazement, for what seemed to me several minutes. Then he turned his gaze away, and was apparently lost in thought; and presently he said, as if to himself, "What an astonishing idea!"

II

"Come," he said, finally, dispelling his reverie and reverting to me with a friendly smile. "If all that is pleasantry, I don't mind being the goat. Really, don't you know that the United States is the most revolution-cursed country in the world? Why do you suppose that spiritual activity in America is virtually non-existent? Simply because we have never yet had that stable order of things which you speak of. Every year of our life for a century and a half we have either been cleaning up after one revolution or getting ready for another. Don't you know that?"

"Well, I don't exactly," I replied, "but I seem to know that either you or this poisonous French coffee has got my brains on the run. A few minutes ago you said we didn't have revolutions enough, and now you say we've had nothing else but. Don't we schedule our revolutions to suit you?"

"We've had only two, but they were big ones," he said, impatiently. "I am for a lot of little ones, and I'm for it because I'm more for getting along without any. Don't bother your head about that paradox; I'll clear it up for you in a moment. First, let's clear up our history in the matter of those revolutions. Remember, to begin with, that a revolution is not always contemporaneous with the rattle of muskets and the roll of drums. These may come before or after. The real revolution takes place when the shift of economic power is effected from one class in society to another. Don't forget that. Well, then, in the colonial days we had a fairly settled order of things and, considering our isolation and the poverty of our cultural apparatus, our spiritual activity gave a mighty good account of itself. Compare our social life and its cultural product with those of any other colonists anywhere in the world, and they are nothing to be ashamed of. We had a line of men, you remember, who could have held their end up with pretty much anybody if the First Revolution had not come along to upset them and divert their energies.

"But the First Revolution did come along, and when it was over its gains had to be consolidated. That's a nice orthodox phrase, and I like to use it. What it really means in this instance is that the issue had to be fought out whether farmer-labour-planting interests should get all four feet in the trough and subordinate the bankers and industrialists, or whether the bankers and industrialists should get all four feet in the trough and exploit agriculture.

"This took almost a century. The financial and manufacturing interests got first innings. They drafted the Constitution, put it through to ratification, and got complete control of the Legislature and Administration for the first ten

213

years. Then they were dislodged in 1800 under Thomas Jefferson, but they still held control of the courts. This leverage, combined with many circumstances, gradually increased their power, but they were put on their back again in 1828 by Andrew Jackson. They got up, dusted themselves off, went at it again, and in the Second Revolution in 1860 they flattened out the agricultural interests for good and all.

"Then the 'consolidation' process had to begin all over again. This time the pious phrase means the arrangement of the terms of exploitation by a victorious social group. Well, I needn't go into details of that period; you have lived through most of it, from the Grant-Belknap — Gould-Fisk — Northern Pacific-Crédit Mobilier kind of thing, down through the South Improvement Company to Fall, Denby, and Sinclair. I don't meant to blow you to a free lesson in American history, but just to bring out the fact that after Britain, the foreign master, was thrown out on his head at Yorktown it took almost exactly eighty years to decide which of two contesting domestic groups should master the other; and after one of the two was pitched out for good and all in 1864 it has taken all the years since then to establish the victor's terms of indemnity and guarantee, and they aren't settled yet.

"I simply want to show you why the United States, spiritually, is in exactly the condition of Soviet Russia, and why the people who look to either country for some great outburst of light and leading are putting down their hopes on a dead card. The Americans eat right, and the Russians don't—not yet. That's the only difference; and the Russians are fast getting around to the American idea that a people who can afford to eat right is a great people. That's the idea behind your precious Mr. Hoover's report on wages."

"But surely," I said, "you won't deny that a diffused material well-being is the basis of all civilization."

"Surely I won't," he replied, "but the basis isn't the structure. You've got forty-seven stories yet to build, and you have to lay out and shape your foundation with reference to your structure. You and I know that, but Mr. Hoover doesn't, and not one American in ten thousand knows it, and the Russians, if they

215

ever knew it, are in a way to forget it as fast
as they can."

He took a notebook from his pocket, and
leafed it over.

"Here it is.   Here's what Walt Whitman
wrote, somewhere about 1870, I think it was—
before you and I were born, anyway.   He was
the Good Grey Poet of Democracy, you understand.   Read it aloud, so I'll be sure you get it."

I took the notebook, and read as follows:

"I say that our New World Democracy, however
great a success in uplifting the masses out of their
sloughs, in materialistic development, products, and
in a certain highly deceptive superficial popular intellectuality, is, so far, an almost complete failure in
its social aspects, and in really grand religious,
moral, literary, and æsthetic results.   In vain do we
march with unprecedented strides to empire so
colossal. . . . It is as if we were somehow being
endowed with a vast and thoroughly appointed
body, and then left with little or no soul."

"Exactly," said my friend, when I had fin-
ished reading the extract, "and if I were
Lunacharsky, I should translate that, print it
at the head of an abstract of United States vital

statistics, and keep it posted in every Russian household.

" '*An almost complete failure in its social aspects.*' Now, why is that? It is because our whole culture has followed the flag, followed it every day of our national life. First, the flag of the revolutionary colonists, then the flag of consolidation, then of revolution again, and now of consolidation again. At this moment every cultural interest in the United States is crowding the flag of consolidation so close that its head is run stone-blind in the folds of it.

"I read the other day that Columbia University had enrolled 35,000 students this year. Now, just ask yourself the one question, *What for?* You can make your own answer—no, you can't, either, for you will be laughing your ribs loose. Then you will go back to Ernest Renan who said, quite a while before Whitman, 'The countries which, like the United States, have created a considerable popular instruction without any serious higher education, will long have to expiate their fault by their intellectual mediocrity, the vulgarity of their manners, their superficial spirit, their failure in general intelligence.'

"A considerable popular instruction, you understand, in whatever is necessary to sell bonds
or motor cars, run a bank or a law office, keep
store, build bridges, and the like—that is, instruction in following the flag of consolidation,
the kind of thing Columbia does so well, none
better. I'm a Columbia man myself, a sort of
black sheep, maybe, but I can still give honour
where honour is due. Education follows the
flag, the arts follow it—think of Pennell and
George Bellows, for instance—literature and
criticism follow it, and so do social life and manners. The reason why there is no such thing
as social conversation in America is only that
every man-jack of us has his mind's eye con-
stantly fixed on the flag and can't think about
anything else. How many men do you know
among us who can talk with you for an hour
about something that is not personal and yet not
symbolized by the flag? I was interested the
other day by something that purported to have
been written by a precocious little brat of a
girl in one of our schools. It is sophomoric
and affected, certainly, and if she were my
daughter, I can see how she'd have had her
behind royally tanned about twice a day from

birth. But she did exactly hit on this point that I am making, that all our social life is degraded to practical barbarism by following the flag of consolidation:

"We are called the pampered, unruly children of the jazz age, but in reality we are the offspring of the machine age, and the cacophony of the band to which we dance is the nerve-tearing bore of electric riveters, the hiss of puddled steel, the almost inaudible whirr of revolving wheels. The machine is turning out dollars and comfort and Ford cars and radios—and the younger generation. Can you stop it—or us?

"There, you see, you have it—the tone set for a complete social life by industry, banking and real-estating, all moiling in the process of consolidating the gains of the Second Revolution."

"Poor old devil!" I said. "No use recommending a drink to a man in your condition. It would take more than French beer to make you see daylight again."

III

"You needn't worry about me," he rejoined. "If anybody doesn't care for that sort of thing,

219

either in America or in Russia, he can mighty easily move out. But we were talking on an impersonal topic, I believe, weren't we?—revolutions and their social effect, I think it was. Well, now I seem to be brought logically down to the paradox of more and better revolutions, so I'll say a word or two about that before we go.

"I know a country that doesn't have any revolutions," he said, tilting his chair back and stretching out comfortably at full length. "The reason why they do not have them is that they are on the brink of one all the time. They make their politicians walk a chalked line. You know, those swine are the same in all countries. They go as far as you let them, but they are the world's prize cowards. Well, in that country the people don't let them go any distance at all. The politicians have got to show 'em, every time, in small things as well as great. I never knew there were so many Missouri people in the world. I remember, fifteen years ago, a friend of mine told the mayor of their biggest town, a fine city of a million or so, that he ought to turn a certain busy thoroughfare into a one-way street. The mayor just threw up his hands, and said, 'If I did that, there would be a revolution!' There would, too, and that mayor wouldn't have lasted as long as a pint of Prohibition busthead at a camp-meeting. He knew the populace would adjourn right down to the City Hall in a body, search him out, and swing him to the handiest lamp-post, and leave him there as a sort of friendly suggestion to his successor to go slow, and not crowd the mourners.

"They are a reasonable people too. It took ten years to introduce traffic regulation in that town. They weren't against it—perfectly intelligent about it and willing to see it tried—and they like it first rate now. Indeed, they were the first people I ever heard of who finally went beyond the authorities, and made them regulate pedestrian traffic, too. But, as I said, they had to be shown every step of the way, and the officials who did the showing handled the job as gingerly as snake-charmers, for fear that the people might take sudden notions. That's the way everything goes in that country, and it is the best place in the world today for a human being to inhabit. They have the finest culture and the most interesting social life that I know. I could spin you yarns by the hour about them—things you simply wouldn't believe. I shan't tell you where all this is, for I don't want Henry Ford to go there—shouldn't mind at all if he'd go himself, you know, but he wouldn't. He'd only send out a lot of poor devils of dependents, and I don't want their blood on my head.

"Think of the Germans and Italians! The Germans are the most admirable of people and very delightful, the Italians the most delightful of people and very admirable. But would you live in either country? Some ignorant bullfrog of a banker comes back to Wall Street all swelled up, and tells us how stable Italy is. Well, so it is, for a banker or a tourist. The trains run on time, the hotels are cleaned up, and all that sort of thing, but nobody's head can hold anything but Fascism. Again you get Fascist art, Fascist social theory, Fascist literature, Fascist music, on the assumption that Fascism is bigger than the human spirit—exactly the counterpart of the assumption that overwhelms you in Russia.

"No, the only intelligent revolution is one that you keep brewing all the time. Why do

222

you suppose Aaron Burr did not contest the election of 1800? Because he knew it wasn't healthy—practically certain to bring on throat trouble. *Marbury* vs. *Madison* would have looked different to John Marshall if he had known there was a rope at the end of it. It's exactly like house-cleaning. Don't you remember how every April the women folks used to turn in and raise the devil for a week, so you couldn't live on the premises? I suppose there is hardly a household in America now that has an old-fashioned spring house-cleaning. They hoe out a little every day, and keep the vacuum cleaner and the disinfectant where they can get their hands on them right away whenever they want them. They don't clean things up, in short; they keep them clean. They are continually organized for quick action, and so they never have to take any.

"That's the way it is with those people I spoke of, who don't have revolutions. They keep themselves perpetually framed up to hang somebody, no matter who, and hence nobody ever gets hanged, and the human spirit enjoys its due degree of freedom. The spiritual atmosphere is not stifling with the filthy miasma

223

sent up by revolution or consolidation. There's
no escaping it, you know; no matter where you
are in America, Russia, Italy, it gets you. The
country I mentioned has the party system in
politics, and you would be amused to see how
carefully the party collisions are localized. The
people know that all hands in all parties are
scoundrels, and they sort of sequestrate the
whole herd, like an old-fashioned red-light dis-
trict. Inside the stockade the politicians can cut
up what obscene gyrations they like, but anyone
caught off the reservation gets it in the neck."

"Pooh!" I said. "This perfectionist tribe of
yours is just like anybody else. People don't
differ."

"Right enough," he replied. "That tribe,
as you call it, has had all this drilled into them
by a long and very special experience. Human
beings learn the art of living only by the in-
delicate means you use when you housebreak a
pup. These people have no peculiar virtues,
except those that were accidentally hammered
into them. But that's neither here nor there.
We were talking about the social effect of revolutions; and I just brought them in for purposes of illustration.

"That social effect is the same everywhere. All sorts of wiseacres are asking what's the matter with Russia, or with America, and are giving us all sorts of answers, mostly wide of the mark, and telling all sorts of stories of what we can expect from the Russia or America of the future, mostly preposterous. Some of them get impatient and scold because they look for the impossible and don't get it. It is no trouble to find out what the matter really is, or to forecast what one can expect, when one gets beyond the mere conventional history of a country's development.

"What on earth is the use of hammering the present generation of Americans and Russians, or poking fun at them for their limitations? Fundamentally, their social philosophy is exactly the same. In a somewhat transfigured sense, their god is their belly. Hence I'm not keen to live among either of them. I am not taken in by that 'certain highly deceptive superficial popular intellectuality' that Whitman speaks of. I know the depth of being from which the cultural life of both countries is lived, and that's enough. But I also know the actual history, the social history, of both countries, and what it leads me to expect is exactly what is before my eyes. In a few hundred years, or a few thousand, their people may learn what revolutions really are, and what their social effect is, and how to dodge both. But I shan't be here then, so meanwhile ———"

But by this time I had had quite enough of my friend's vagaries, and I went my way, wondering rather sadly at the debility produced upon a really brilliant intellect, as he was in the old days, by two years' sojourn among the poor brainsick creatures of the Soviets.

To Youngsters of Easy Means

I

W_{HEN} I was a boy the American millionaire and his impulsive prodigality were already good stage-properties; his generosity towards everything he believed in was as great, as easily touched, and often as spectacular as it is now. Nor was he behindhand in patronizing the fine arts, at least for the embellishment of his own surroundings. He built elaborate houses, some of which it is safe to say were in certain respects truly remarkable, and he ornamented them with pictures bought at inflated prices which he paid without wincing—and concerning a good many of these, too, it is becoming to speak with like indefiniteness and reserve. These ventures often, perhaps, reflected the easy indulgence of feminine fancies and foibles, which early became proverbial of him, but in many cases—I believe in most—they came out of the more admirable sentiment that while pretty much anything would do first rate for him, nothing could be too good for the folks; and the thicker the

227

folks chose to lay it on, the grimmer his satisfaction in seeing them do it. This satisfaction
was sometimes about all the poor man got; he
was often oppressed by his surroundings, and
found it hard to expand his simpler tastes to
meet their demands. Mr. Howells sketched his
type well in *The Rise of Silas Lapham*, and in
an earlier day Mr. Curtis also sketched it well in
The Potiphar Papers.

The primeval millionaire's interest in the arts,
however, reached no further than this. He
would do anything in reason or out of reason
by way of providing gimcrackery to satisfy the
notions of his wife and daughters, but he did
not regard art in itself as something incumbent
on him to reverence and to promote. *L'art
pour l'art* was distinctly out of his line. Perhaps the arts were all very well for women,
who were strange creatures anyway, and hardly
to be understood. In his practical view of
women (he being a Victorian of deepest dye)
some were superhuman, others subhuman, but
none human. Yet even for women, devotion
to the arts could be overdone, and the effect
sometimes was to make things uncomfortable.
Like Silas Lapham, he remembered his earlier

surroundings, the rag carpets that his mother made, the bric-à-brac and chromos, the stout rush-bottomed chairs, and so on, and he thought a little rebelliously of how much easier they all were to get along with. For one thing, then, and perhaps primarily, the promotion of the arts meant pushing all the real comforts of personal environment into yet more hopeless inaccessibility, and he instinctively resented the idea. One can criticise this sentiment in the abstract, probably, but all things considered, it is not easy to disparage those who had it. In them, on the contrary, considering all their circumstances, it seemed pretty sound and natural, and its conservatism savored of a wholesome simplicity. After all, the arts were exotic to America, and these men behaved extremely well towards a rather busy and importunate obtrusion of them upon their intimate life. If unselfishness be the first instinct of a gentleman, probably the unpretentious figures of Mr. Potiphar and Silas Lapham will stand pretty well up in the category with Roland's and Sir Philip Sidney's.

Our typical rich man regarded the arts, moreover, as essentially European, and a devotion

to them as not only negatively un-American, but
as a positive and culpable hankering after the
insignia of an alien civilization.   This was not
the worst; he regarded this civilization as effete,
decadent, effeminate.   Even this was not the
worst.   Aside from the nationalist view, artistic
pursuits and interests related themselves directly
in his mind with a distinct possibility of personal
peril and humiliation.   Too deep a feeling for
the arts might easily open the way for the fetid
fascinations of European social life to assert
themselves upon his wife and children.   His
boys might suffer undermining of their sturdy
American morale.   Most undesirable of all,
his girls might find a bond of sentimental com-
munion with some utterly impracticable and ob-
jectionable foreign man of title, eager to feather
his nest.   The Marquis de Vautrien, the Duca
del Scioccone, and the Viscount Dedbroke stood
continually before his mind's eye as sinister
figures, suave, ingratiating, impecunious, immoral, deceitful, and desperately wicked. When
he thought of the arts, he thought of them;
and when he thought of them, he ground his
teeth, and expressed his emotions of the moment in a flow of spirited profanity.

II

Perhaps it was the Marquis, the Duca, the Viscount, and the deportmental exactions of the new house that carried the rich man of my boyhood a little beyond his predecessors in an impatient wariness of the arts. The prosperous American of earlier days, especially in New England, had a little different attitude towards art, at least when art assailed him in the guise of a domestic issue. Once in a generation or so, one of the God-fearing, whale-catching, rum-distilling, close-fisted Puritan families of the New England coast would produce a black sheep who did not want to go to sea, and cared nothing for rum and whales, but instead had a passion for beauty and harmony. He wanted to paint pictures or sing, learn the violin, study architecture, or write books. It was a fearful blow to the family's pride. The neighbors, hearing of this appalling calamity, would look at one another with blank faces, and say, "Isn't it awful?" But the stricken family would swallow the disgrace, and if they found their erring son actually obdurate and beyond entreaty, they would grimly and prayerfully stake him. They

would send him to Europe to study, devoutly
hoping he might soon get it all out of his system, come home, and go before the mast in the
honorable tradition of his ancestors. Thus it
happened that in those days America showed
some well-developed ability and talent; not
much, perhaps, but more than one would expect, I think, considering the circumstances of
the country.

But in my childhood, there was nothing like
this in the life of the fine old buccaneering type
of millionaire who went mostly in his shirt
sleeves in the summertime, and worked four-
teen hours every day until Satan foreclosed on
his flagitious enterprise of cabbaging everything
that was not spiked down. He distinctly did
not regard subsidizing a promising youth,
whether his own or somebody else's, to learn
to paint pictures or play the fiddle, as a good
investment. Propose it to him, and before you
got the words out of your mouth he would be
jumping three feet high. I speak with authority, for I knew several very rich men of
this type. My father was a clergyman who
had a parish for twelve years in a virgin lum-
ber-country, and his congregation comprised a

dozen such, maybe more. I studied their ways
with immense amusement and considerable ad-
miration. They were the only very rich men
I ever knew, and I rather regret the disappearance of their type. Perhaps our modern man of
wealth has as vivid, distinct, and forceful a personality as theirs, but I doubt it. Looking over
the contemporary rich man at long range, I question whether Satan would think him much of
an acquisition, or be in any particular hurry to
gather him in. There was no discount on those
earlier brethren, however. They were lurid
personages, who could be counted on to make
their surroundings extremely lively wherever
they found themselves, and each one who
dropped off was just so much clear gain to the
social life of the lower regions.

So, if it were a question of setting up an
art-gallery, endowing a conservatory of music,
boosting the theatre or opera, doing a good turn
for literature, or staking individual talent on its
way to an exiguous self-support, the millionaire
of my early days would count himself out with
emphasis. But curiously, at this same period a
great deal was being done with the arts in an
amateur way. In the town that I have been

233

speaking of, for instance, where my father's parish was, there was a most extraordinary development of amateur music. In particular, I have never since then seen the coincidence of so many really fine male voices in a town of its size, and all with fine amateur cultivation. There were many good woman singers too, and one woman, I remember rather vividly, the wife of a local shoe-dealer, got marvellous and beautiful effects out of whistling. We were a Lake town, sixty miles from a railway, and when an old-fashioned Michigan winter closed down on us, we were completely isolated, and thrown on our own resources for entertainment, for a good long six months. All these people worked hard at music then, individually and in a sort of loosely organized choral society, and they did some excellent things with it.

The country was at this time, moreover, just on the fag-end of the period when young men at large were rather gingerly encouraged to have an "accomplishment," and well-to-do young women had one or more as matter-of-course. There was a good deal about this that was afflictive, and a later generation recalls it with merited raillery. Mark Twain speaks of

234

the beribboned guitar standing in a corner of the Southern parlor—a guitar capable, he says, of playing the Spanish Fandango by itself, if you gave it a start. As I remember, however, most of the acute distress caused me by the amateur musicians of that day was due to the *répertoires.* Young ladies who played the piano were likely to spread themselves on a considerable line of "descriptive music," like "The Battle of Prague," or to exude sentiment over the ilk of Leybach's Fifth Nocturne. The vocalist's range of choice was even more poverty-stricken, being ninety-eight per cent bilge-water English ballads, and the remaining two per cent Scotch and Irish, with an occasional variant of early American, such as "Home, Sweet Home," and "The Swanee River." I have heard many glorious voices and many very decent musical instincts wasted evening after evening on things like "In the Gloaming," "The Blue Alsatian Mountains," "O Fair Dove, O Fond Dove," and "Alice, Where Art Thou?"

As much can be said of the common run of china-painting, work in crayon, charcoal, oil and water-color, leather-burning, hammering metals, and so on, that prevailed in that period.

235

I am quite of my younger contemporaries' mind in deriding the puniness of artistic aspiration represented by all this. I know more about it than they do, indeed, for I have suffered under it, and they have not. Poetry, too—amateur poetry—I have fit, bled, and died over reams of lushy poetry. So I am not dwelling regretfully upon the disappearance of that epoch, nor do I seriously wish it back again. Far from it. I am merely remarking the fact that in a day when it was impossible to get money to promote the practice of the arts in a competent way, and to make sound taste prevail, a great many people were actually practising them as best they could in a misdirected and hamstrung way, and employing sometimes a very fine talent to make bad taste prevail.

III

At the present time, I seem to see an interesting reversal of this state of things. My observations may be superficial and inaccurate, for I have been for years entirely out of any kind of social life in America, and all manner of things that I know nothing about may be going on there. Quite obviously, however, the arts

236

are lavishly patronized—patronized, I mean, in the sense of direct subsidy. Every few days, it seems, one hears of some great gift or endowment to promote them. Sir Thomas Beecham was lately quoted as saying that one American friend of his spent as much money annually to keep up an orchestra in his town as all England put together raised for like purposes. I do not doubt it. When one reads publications devoted to the various arts, as curiosity has led me to do for some time as regularly as I could get my hands on them, one is impressed by the enormous amount of money laid out in these ways.

I should say, too, that there would be relatively little difficulty in finding subsidies to almost any extent for promising individuals, although it is true, I think, that our rich men do not as yet go in as much for this form of patronage, which is the oldest, and still seems to get the best results, as they do for the institutional form. For my part, I wish they would do more with it. I know that if I were a rich man I would do precious little with endowing institutions, and content myself with nosing out individuals of the right sort, and endowing

237

them.   But aside from method, in so far as
national progress in the arts can be measured by
the gross of money given to promote it, America is stepping faster than any country on earth
has ever stepped.

At the same time, I notice that relatively
much less amateur work is being done in any
of the arts except one—literature—than was
done under the old régime when I was a boy.
The arts have come to be a matter concerning
two classes only: a professional class and a non-
participating public.   Most of the immense
amount of writing that is being done has a professional or semi-professional turn, being done
in some kind of forlorn hope of some day making money by it.   The amateur "accomplishment" in the arts has largely disappeared, except
in dancing.   Nearly all young Americans dance,
and most of them extremely well.   The young-
ster of my day, especially the young woman,
had, as a rule, a preposterously imperfect idea of
what an accomplishment was, and what it was
for; but their successors, instead of retaining
and valuing the accomplishment, straightening
out its theory and improving its practice, have
tended rather, I think, to drop it altogether.

238

Thus it is that while people today know far more about really good music, good pictures, good sculpture, than the people of my time, and are possibly more interested in them, their knowledge and interest are pretty strictly of a non-participating kind. They themselves do not sing, play, daub or gouge. They patronize staunchly, look and listen attentively, applaud enthusiastically. All credit to them for this. But a non-participating interest can never quite attain to the quality of a participating interest, and is almost always something quite different and much less satisfying. No amount of time spent in sitting on the grand-stand will get one into the innards of a ball game, and give one the gratifying feel of the skill involved in certain plays, like a little practical apprenticeship out on the sand-lots in Mr. Briggs's "days of real sport." I played ball for eleven years myself, and speak whereof I know. Similarly, no one gets the instinctive appraisal, the true and exhilarating *feel* of fine points in tone-production and in breath-control, in line and color, like him who has ever so little, perhaps, but with love and intelligence, done his bit at warbling and smearing. No listener can appreciate the "in-

239

side play" in a suite of Bach, like one who had tried to drum it out himself. Therefore it follows, I think, that the general climate of opinion and feeling which prevails in a participating public is higher in quality, and much more conducive to the true and effective promotion of art, than that which prevails in a non-participating public. It stands to reason that the real status of musical art in a community is to be estimated by the number of people who practise it, and not by the box-office returns from concerts and the opera; just as the status of cleanliness is not to be estimated by the amount of plumbing sold, but by the number of people who wash.

IV

But whether so or not, there can be no doubt that participation is more fun, and this is the only point that I mean to dwell on. I have no thought of making a plea for the future of the arts in America. What really started me out on these reflections was the news lately conveyed to me in a private letter, that in one of our Western cities several business men, well along in years and of large wealth, have secretly, clandestinely, surreptitiously, and insidiously banded themselves together to study drawing and painting in a practical way, by doggedly plugging away with brush and pencil, under a teacher. Here, I thought at once, is the real thing! Here is America in earnest! It is commendable to have learned how to give money prodigally for the support of the arts, but the genuine fun begins when the same people who give the money make up their minds to jump in themselves, tackle the actual practice of some art, and make what they can of it in a strictly amateur way, and "on the side."

Incidentally, it is good for art; it is the one thing needful, really, because, as I said, it helps most to engender a congenial atmosphere, and it also puts into effect the best insurance against waste of money. This handful of Western business men are really in the best way to protect their investments. When some one tells them cock-and-bull stories about the colossal innovations of Schmierpinsel in Vienna, and the revolutionary ideas of Barbenfeu in Paris, and how these have completely effaced all traditions, and sent Rembrandt and Frans Hals back to the woodpile, they will be in a position to look the matter over intelligently for themselves—

an advantage which some of our contemporary private collectors appear to have missed most lamentably. But apart from this, they are laying up a resource of incalculable delight for themselves, and that is the great thing.

In the new social order, the leisured class— those, that is, who can command leisure if they wish it—stand towards art in somewhat the relation of the old aristocracy; and in Europe one sees the extraordinary leavening power of the talents which were cultivated by such of the aristocracy as had them. As talents, they may have been unpretentious, rather pleasant than robust, but they tended powerfully towards the diffusion of an agreeable and amiable life; and because they did this, one cannot help thinking that they made life amiable primarily for those who exercised them. The poetry of the Grand Duke Constantine connotes a more agreeable life than that which (without pretending to know) one instinctively associates with the thought of the late Judge Gary, for example. Seeing in Brussels the beautiful paintings and sculpture done by the Count de Lalaing—not great, I think, but very lovely—one thinks of him as a happy man, and one would like to have

known him. *Noblesse oblige*—men like these
seem really to have made something of their
position and opportunities *all around,* and there
is no happiness to match what one gets out of
doing that.

There is much room in America for the exercise of a merely *pleasant* talent, if it be exercised in true taste and for no motive but the
love of it, for money and leisure are so abundant
—one has to be in Europe to realize how relatively abundant they are, and to understand
how much happiness a little intelligent self-
direction could produce from them. I know a
solicitor in London, as pure a type as the one
that Gilbert and Sullivan put on the stage in
"Patience," who plays Bach for an hour every
evening when he comes home from his office.
In talking about Flemish folk-ways lately with
a Belgian engineer, a man busy with his profession from dawn to dark, mention was made
of a couple of interesting old Flemish songs.
He sat down at the piano, rattled off a rather
intricate accompaniment, and sang them for me
most agreeably, and with the unmistakable taste
of the cultivated amateur. The Royal Opera
would never put him on for his singing, or the

243

Conservatory for his playing, and he would not have the least wish to go on for either. He simply had the view of the arts, so general in Europe, so uncommon in America, as something for anyone to take a hand in, naturally and easily, because one loves them, because they are familiar and domestic assets for making life agreeable and amiable for oneself—with no thought of using them on the chance of money or fame, or for anyone's pleasure but one's own, and least of all with any repulsive delirium of vanity about "self-expression."

v

Americans are inclined to be a little impatient of a critic who does not offer what they call "practical proposals"; one, that is, who does not pretend to do all their thinking for them, furnish all their initiative, and diagram all their actions, thus imposing on them no harder task than the rather mechanical one of putting one foot before the other. For certain reasons hardly worth recounting here, I have always been a little diffident about making practical proposals. Still, if it helps to show that one is in earnest, one might perhaps venture a little way with

244

them. To the men who now give money so liberally to promote the arts, the men who might be thought, perhaps, to be looking at the arts a little wistfully—men like the late Mr. Munsey, for example—I would say, If you wish really to promote the arts, keep on with the money, but also sell one of your motor-cars, buy a second-hand piano or some paint or crayons or modelling-clay, and get somebody to show you what to do with it. You will have a great deal of fun, more fun than ever you had in your life, and you may incidentally turn up some aptitude inside yourself that you never suspected of lurking there.

But there is another class of candidates for my magisterial attentions, and with them I shall be even more specific. These are the young men and women who are not doing much at the moment but amuse themselves, who feel some faint stirrings of a desire to do something a little more important, who think they may possibly have some small ability in some department of art, and who also have enough money —or may have it for the asking—to see them through pretty much anything that they wish to attempt. America is full of just such young-

245

sters. Their surroundings are rather against
their doing more with themselves than they are
doing, yet a good many of them are vaguely
dissatisfied and would like a job, if they could
find one that they felt really counted. Naturally, they do not want something that keeps
them merely marking time, or that will show
no particular achievement when it is done, but
they are ready to look disinterestedly at something that is an actual challenge, and if they
liked it, they would be willing to put their backs
into tackling it.

Well, the fields of art are full of jobs—great
jobs—that ought to be done, that would bring
endless satisfaction to those who did them, but
that can never be done except by people who
can afford to do them, because there is no
money in them and never will be. Here, it has
always seemed to me, is the leisured young
American's chance, and I cannot understand
how he has managed to miss it for so long. In
the sciences, I notice, he has long ago caught on
in precisely the same adventurous way he might
catch on in the arts. He is in the laboratories,
he is on all sorts of scientific expeditions, toil-
ing away at his own expense in enterprises that

he knows will never bring him the worth of a copper cent in anything but the exhilarating sense of a great job greatly done. Exactly the same chance is waiting for him in the arts.

Take it in the one department of art with which I am, perhaps, a little acquainted. There is not a publisher in America worth his salt who does not know of at least a dozen great and distinguished pieces of literary work waiting to be done, which can never be done until some one comes along who can afford to do them. I could myself name offhand a dozen such. In my casual talks with publishers about various pieces of work that needed doing, the first question has always been, Who can do it? and the next one was, How will he keep himself going meanwhile? My conviction is that the only procedure that will get this kind of work satisfactorily produced is the one that produced the great Flemish pictures, or the one that now gets analogous results in science—*i.e.*, training people to produce it; and because there is no money in such work when it is produced, the only people eligible to be trained are the ones I am addressing.

The procedure is as follows—and here I

247

hope I shall be specific enough to meet fully the American yearning for practical proposals. Suppose these paragraphs that I am writing fall into the hands of a young man or woman, such as I have described, who takes stock of himself and decides he wishes to try his edge on a real job in literature. Let him go to some publisher with this book in his hand, and say, "You see what this writer says. Well, now, my general training is so-and-so; my leanings, as far as I can make them out, are so-and-so; and I have so-many dollars a year to live on while I am on one of these jobs that this essay says are going begging. What about it?"

Then the publisher, if, as I say, he be worth his salt, as none too many of them are—tell it not in Gath!—will bring forth a line of subjects that will make the young person's mouth water. They will agree on one, and the publisher will say, "Now, the thing to do is for you to go to So-and-so, just as Rubens went in his youth to van Noort and van Veen. He is quite a fellow in that line, so go to him and stand him up on the carpet, get him to talk it over with you, put an eye on your work once in a while, stiffen up your backbone, and in a gen-

248

eral way hold the bull-whip over you until you get your gait."

The other arts hold as many and as great possibilities which remain to be developed by the same line of procedure. I myself happen to know of one most spicy adventure in the line of the graphic arts, which calls for just the resourcefulness and quickness of mind that Americans are supposed to have. It might turn out to be a dud, but how many exploratory and experimental scientific undertakings turn out that way! Any really competent expert in that line knows of others; any really competent musician knows of a dozen lying here and there in the theory, history, or practice of music; and so on. The thing is to get these experts to stand and deliver, as they will do if they are put under reasonable conviction of the young person's seriousness of purpose, and to convince them of this is a good preliminary test of the enthusiasm and pertinacity of American youth.

THE END